"Empowering, encouraging, heartwrenchingly honest at times, Betsy's story of the emotional trauma and abandonment she endured along her journey and her incredible hard work towards recovery is a must-read for any person struggling with finding their voice. The descriptions of her childhood, college, law school years, and her adult life are so vivid and captivating, the reader almost feels they are rallying alongside Betsy. This book is a gift of hope she is sharing with all those who know the isolation of an eating disorder."

—Denise Glickman, MD

"Betsy's story is one that needs to be told. Her lived experience and continued eating disorder recovery needs to be heard not only by women in midlife, but also as a 'should-read' for girls with disordered eating thoughts who are in the competitive sports arena."

—Randi Beranbaum, MS, RD, LDN

THE LONGEST MATCH

Rallying to Defeat an
Eating Disorder in Midlife

BETSY BRENNER

Visit our website at
www.StillwaterPress.com
for more information.

First Stillwater River Publications Edition

ISBN: 978-1-955123-08-2

Library of Congress Control Number: 2021907902

1 2 3 4 5 6 7 8 9 10

Written by Betsy Brenner
Published by Stillwater River Publications,
Pawtucket, RI, USA.

Publisher's Cataloging-In-Publication Data
(Prepared by The Donohue Group, Inc.)

Names: Brenner, Betsy, author.
Title: The longest match : rallying to defeat an eating
disorder in midlife / Betsy Brenner.
Description: First Stillwater River Publications edition. |
Pawtucket, RI, USA : Stillwater River Publications, [2021]
Identifiers: ISBN 9781955123082
Subjects: LCSH: Brenner, Betsy. | Eating disorders--
Patients--Biography. | Middle-aged women--Biography. |
LCGFT: Autobiographies.
Classification: LCC RC552.E18 B74 2021 |
DDC 616.85260092--dc23

To Jeff,
who has made my dreams come true.
You are my everything.
To Rebecca, Matthew and Alexis,
our most precious blessings.

You've always had the power, my dear.
You just had to learn it for yourself.

—Glinda the Good Witch
The Wizard of Oz (1939)

CONTENTS

FOREWORD

Imagine a ball made out of streamer paper, the kind you string across a room for birthday parties. Imagine the paper is wrapped in layers, like a ball of yarn. Now imagine that buried between the layers of delicate paper are small trinkets waiting to be revealed as the ball unwinds. I played a game with a ball like this one New Year's Eve. The experience reminds me of what it is like to work with someone who has an eating disorder. The client arrives in my office, neatly and tightly wrapped in their illness. Rushed or abrupt attempts to unwrap, easily rip the paper and thwart the process. Successful treatment involves a slow, shared process of gently unrolling the ball to reveal pieces of information among the many layers. First, uncovering, then identifying and finally understanding these pieces are critical to achieve recovery. It is hard to change something if you don't know what it is, or why it is, or how it came to be.

An eating disorder is a functional system that develops to protect an individual from injuries and hurts from which they have felt powerless or inadequate in their ability to protect themselves. The individual's vulnerability in key relationships where they have felt hurt, shamed, unloved, or insufficient, unconsciously leads to a redirection of energy to a goal and aim that can be controlled. Thus, by following rigid rules around eating, food, or calories, the individual creates a system by which they can attempt to feel sufficient. Each day they manage to restrict their food intake, or refuse all sweets, there is a hint of achievement, sufficiency, control, and transient relief from the fear of inadequacy. By engaging in this internal tug of war, the individual unwittingly replaces the vulnerability they feel in their relationship with others, with an all-consuming relationship with themselves.

This new relationship has the illusion of control but, as the rules that comprise an eating disorder are so rigid and unforgiving, the feeling is one of always being at risk for failure. It is as though life is lived running at the very back of a treadmill and any sneeze or momentary distraction will cause you to fall off. There is no moment to relax, no option for imperfection. Ironically, this perpetual and unrelenting potential for failure feels nothing like mastery, agency or control to the individual.

When I first met Betsy, she was very tightly wrapped. She knew that on paper her life appeared perfect. She had three smart and healthy children, she had a loving husband, a sport she enjoyed and excelled at, a strong community and good friends, and meaningful endeavors in her coaching and grief work. But with me, in the beginning, she was guarded and defensive. Her history of hurt and past experiences of emotional neglect required that she not show vulnerability and hide her needs. Despite her incredible community she reported feeling lonely because her emotional needs were often unmet. She knew that her eating disorder was a concern to others, she knew that it limited her ability to be close to others, but she didn't know why or how much. Consciously she was clear that she wanted to recover; unconsciously, she guarded what lay beneath those delicate layers: anger, hurt, and needs.

The careful unspooling of each layer with Betsy has been a remarkable experience. I have seen her recognize experiences, emotions, needs and begin to feel them fully, and I have watched her share her feelings more authentically and openly with important people in her life. Betsy's commitment to sharing her story to help others with eating disorders has been an impactful part of her own healing process. It is notable that she and I had many lengthy debates before she was willing to even share with one friend that she had an eating disorder. The progression from this first telling, to her courage to tell her complete story in this book, has been inspiring to behold.

Betsy's generosity of spirit towards others has fueled her ability to be more generous with herself. The care and dedication she has directed towards writing this memoir has brought her closer to the difficult pieces of her early life that were embedded at the innermost part of that fragile paper ball. As she unwrapped, layer by layer, Betsy realized that many of her hurts were not due to her own insufficiency, and that the guilt she felt for having needs was not warranted.

Working with individuals who have eating disorders can be challenging because while they may want to recover, they also do not want to give up their familiar means of feeling secure and protected, that is, their eating disorder. As the therapist, that can mean I am an aggressor, trying to wrestle my client away from their protected patterns. Betsy and I certainly had our moments of tug-of-war but we both always understood why we persevered. Her commitment to recovery, her investment in our relationship and the process, and her desire to learn ways to care for herself and others has been a privileged journey. I know that others will benefit from Betsy's journey to make progress in unspooling their own.

—Emily Spurrell, Ph.D.
Clinical Psychologist
Assistant Clinical Professor
Warren Alpert Medical School,
Brown University

ACKNOWLEDGMENTS

Thank you to Dr. June Alexander of Australia for her professional editing, mentoring, and guidance. Her warmth, encouragement, and support were felt from the other side of the world through every step of writing my memoir.

Thank you to Emily Spurrell, Ph.D., my therapist extraordinaire, for her professional insight, care, and compassion. Her astute skills, honesty, encouragement, and support have been instrumental in both my recovery and in writing my memoir. The journey continues . . .

Thank you to Margo Maine, Ph.D., FAED, CEDS, for reading my manuscript and believing in the importance of sharing my story. Dr. Maine has over 35 years of experience in the eating disorder field including co-founding her private practice, Maine & Weinstein in West Hartford, Connecticut, authoring several books in the field of eating disorders, and speaking nationally and internationally with expertise in eating disorders in mid-life. In addition to being a distinguished clinical psychologist, writer, and speaker, Dr. Maine is a founding member of both the National Eating Disorders Association and the Academy for Eating Disorders.

Thank you to Beth Mayer, LICSW, for reading my manuscript and supporting me as a recovery speaker, writer, and peer support mentor. I first met Beth when she was the esteemed Executive Director of the Multi-Service Eating Disorders Association (MEDA). Beth is a licensed independent clinical social worker in private practice with over 35 years of experience in treating eating disorders.

Thank you to Grace, my dietitian, who went above and beyond in her care and support. She believed in me when I had trouble believing in myself and taught me important lessons, not only about nutrition, but also about life. Even the painful lessons were essential for my journey to physical and emotional health and well-being. I will always be grateful for her compelling role in my recovery.

Thank you to Randi Beranbaum, MS, RD, LDN, Founder and Director of be Collaborative Care in Providence, Rhode Island. Her vision, dedication, and tireless efforts for the benefit of those affected by eating disorders is truly inspiring. I appreciate all of her support and her giving me the opportunity to help others.

Thank you to past and present members of my health care team and other special people in my life who have helped me on my journey to wellness in body, mind, and spirit.

Thank you to my family members and close friends who have read chapters of my manuscript and provided valuable feedback and tremendous support.

Thank you to my dear friend, Denise Glickman, MD, who inspires me beyond words. Her friendship, honesty, love, and support help me to continue to grow into the best version of myself.

And lastly, but most importantly, I thank Jeff, my husband and best friend, for his emotional investment in this project and for typing every single word of my manuscript, often at the end of his long workdays. I am grateful for his love and support each and every day.

INTRODUCTION

This memoir takes the reader on my life's journey from childhood through the 2020 pandemic. My story is about innocence and trauma, love and heartache, anxiety and peace, reticence and voice, joy and sadness. My suburban childhood, privileged education, tennis career, law school, marriage, and motherhood are explored. More profoundly, this is a story about healing in mid-life from childhood trauma and growing into the healthiest version of myself.

I experienced significant challenges amidst privilege and opportunity, including anxiety, depression, grief, loss, adult onset asthma, and ultimately a mid-life eating disorder. My eating disorder was both the culmination of facing challenges, as well as the catalyst for healing. My story details what triggered the challenges and my long road to recovery.

In 1970, when I was seven years old, my parents divorced, leaving a sad inner child who was unable to express any emotions. Mom went on with life as if nothing had happened, so that is what I learned and tried to do. As a result, I believed that being strong meant always being positive and unemotional.

My parents loved me, but because of their own issues, they were not always able to provide the unconditional love I craved. In many ways, I had a privileged childhood, but I grew up feeling that I had to be perfect in order to earn my parents' love and approval. In striving for perfection in the classroom and on the tennis court, I was not only unable to express emotions, but I also felt guilty for even thinking a negative thought. I had no voice and continued to internalize the difficult emotions. The tennis court became my escape from anxiety and negative feelings. My inability to feel and express how I was feeling meant I was not equipped to cope with complicated grief following my parents' early deaths.

My diaries from childhood and adulthood provide a wide lens to the past. I experienced anxiety and mild depression from a young age, though neither condition was diagnosed until adult onset asthma developed in my early 40s. Managing this chronic physical disease exacerbated my anxiety and frequent flare ups made me feel out of control.

Around this time, I returned to tennis after not playing for 20 years. During my break from tennis, I attended law school, married, and had three children. After returning to tennis, I lost weight I did not need to lose. The tennis court once again became my sanctuary and I developed an intense fear of gaining weight.

My journals revealed both a heightened focus on weight and body image and a consistent mindset connecting food intake and exercise. However, an eating disorder did not fully develop until around the time of my asthma diagnosis. When asthma flare ups kept me off the court, I began restricting my food intake. I was diagnosed with anorexia after losing too much weight and becoming consumed by thoughts about food and exercise. The eating disorder helped me to cope with a fear of gaining weight and also with the anxiety from my frequent asthma flare ups which left me feeling out of control.

My recovery journey required me to get in touch with 40 years of internalizing difficult emotions—not only as a result of my parents' divorce but also from their devastating cancer deaths a decade apart. I was an adult orphan by the age of 33. Prior to their untimely deaths I was able to experience two good years with each of them after years of complicated relationships.

In recovery, I literally needed permission to feel my feelings and get in touch with suppressed emotions. I needed to let my guard down and be vulnerable. This required undoing everything that had been ingrained in me from a young age. I had been raised to equate vulnerability with weakness.

Through my recovery journey I found my voice. I learned that taking care of myself and my needs, with self-love and compassion, is essential. Now in my 50s, I am healing from the emotional trauma of my childhood and young adulthood. I can be my authentic self and make my health and well-being a priority. I can feel both the joy of abundant blessings and feel sadness without guilt. In recovery, I had to learn how to nourish and nurture my body, mind and spirit.

Though there were many twists and turns along the way, I was able to navigate the road to recovery with professional care and the support of those closest to me. I have learned many lessons and am excited to see where my journey takes me next. We are never too old to be a work in progress!

—Betsy Brenner

Owning our stories and loving ourselves through the process is the bravest thing we'll ever do.

—*The Gifts of Imperfection*
Brené Brown, Ph.D., LMSW
Research Professor, University of Houston

CHAPTER I

The Innocence of My Early Childhood: Memories From Suburbia

My story begins in 1963 in suburban Rochester, New York. I grew up in the town of Brighton, an affluent suburb filled with residential neighborhoods and some of the best public schools in all of New York State. There were tree-lined streets, homes of all sizes with neatly trimmed hedges, yards, swing sets, and tall white street-lights that came on at dusk.

The small commercial town center was called Twelve Corners. In addition to the fire station, one of two Middle Schools, and the High School, there were several stores. Super Duper was a small market where we went when we needed just a few things. The larger supermarkets, Star and Wegmans, were in Pittsford, the next town over. Howard Johnson's, with its orange roof, was a place for lunch out or to order an ice cream treat at the counter. There were always tempting chocolate lollipops on a stand at the cash register. Altiers was the family owned shoe store where staff measured our feet by standing on a metal foot measuring device and then brought out several boxes from the back room to try on. The usual categories were sneakers, school shoes, and party shoes. A ritual of late spring was getting new white sandals as we only wore white footwear from Memorial Day to Labor Day.

Next to Altiers was Neisners, a variety store with everything from school supplies to a well-stocked candy display. A short distance from Twelve Corners was the Town Hall which also housed the town police station and the Brighton library. During story time at the library, the children's librarian passed out Oreo cookies at the conclusion of the morning's story. My sister and I loved picking out our birthday cakes at French Road Bakery where they always gave us a tiny free frosted sugar cookie. There were tootsie pops at the Dry Cleaners where a friendly lady named Connie did any necessary alterations for us and always warmly commented on how much we had grown. When we accompanied Mom to the hairdresser, I remember glass coke bottles, and trays of delicious cookies at Christmas time.

Chilson's Pharmacy was where my Dad picked up the *New York Times* every Sunday and when I would accompany him, I got to choose a new flair pen to bring home. They came in so many colors and I loved adding to my collection to use for my colorful drawings. We also got the daily Rochester paper, the *Democrat & Chronicle*. On Sunday mornings, Dad and I read the funnies together in our cozy living room. We used silly putty to pick up the colorful comics off the paper and excitedly saw the comics appear on the putty.

On warm summer nights, Dad grilled meat outside on the domed Weber charcoal grill. On many cold winter weekends, we headed to our ski club less than an hour away. As a young child, I would ski down the mountain between my Dad's legs while my non-skiing mom waited for us in the lodge. My favorite memory of those ski days was the big round sprinkled sugar cookies from Fox's Delicatessen. I would have to eat a certain number of bites of my corned beef on rye before I could have my cookie.

Mom always said that Dad collected club memberships. So, in addition to the ski club, we went to on winter weekends, we also had a club we could go to in the summer months which had an inviting pool, snack bar, lounge chairs, tennis courts, squash courts, a bowling alley and a fancy restaurant. The pool opened on Memorial Day and we could hardly wait for that first swim following the big parade that marched right past the club's entrance.

On paper, my parents seemed perfect for each other. Alice Anne Denonn, born in 1936, was raised in Brooklyn Heights, New York. Her father, Lester Eugene Denonn, was a successful Wall Street lawyer, walking over the

Brooklyn Bridge to and from work each day. He was also a philosopher and writer, and he had a passion for exploring bookstores and adding to his personal library. He met my grandmother, Bess Schwimmer Denonn, when they were 12 years old. She was college educated and worked as a teacher before having children. My maternal grandparents were active in their Brooklyn Heights community and eventually travelled the world. Somewhere in my basement I have a box of the love letters they wrote to one another when my grandfather was a student at Cornell University. I also have their travel journals and a small stuffed koala which they brought me from Australia. They were devoted grandparents and I have fond memories of visiting them in Brooklyn as well as their visits to Rochester, especially for birthdays and holidays. Grandma Bess was always impeccably dressed with a matching velvet headband and purses carefully color coordinated with her shoes. Grandpa Lester never was without a tie and jacket. They were happily married for 60 years, living out the vow of "til death do us part."

Mom, and her older brother Andrew, had a relatively privileged childhood, including attending local private schools. Mom went on to graduate from Smith College with a degree in Government and started graduate work at Columbia University before leaving to go to work for her local Congressman in Washington, DC. Mom always said that her dream was to become the first female United States Senator from New York. She never planned to get married or have children. Her "all or nothing" thinking apparently started early on, and it certainly impacted my life. Her plans dramatically changed in her early twenties when she met my father at a New York State political convention in the summer of 1958.

At that time, Richard Lewis Epstein was a young lawyer at a prestigious law firm in Rochester. Born in 1930, he grew up in New York City, attended private school, graduated from Amherst College, and Yale Law School.

My father's father, Harry Browdy Epstein, was a prominent lawyer in New York City. My father's mother, Sarah Bussell Epstein, known as Sally, was a Kindergarten teacher. I never met my grandfather as he died well before my parents were married. Grandma Sally left New York City for Florida when I was a young girl, so I did not see her often. My paternal grandparents each came from large families, so Dad grew up with his older brother Robert and many first cousins.

After meeting at this summer political convention, my parents had a whirlwind romance, got engaged in September, and had a small elegant wedding at a fancy New York City hotel in December 1958. They honeymooned at the magnificent Greenbrier Resort in Sulphur Springs, West Virginia before starting their married life in an apartment in Rochester. Dad continued his work as a lawyer, specializing in Labor Law on behalf of management and served on many local Boards, including Planned Parenthood. Mom worked in what is now called Human Resources at a local hospital and became very involved in her new community. They both remained active in politics at both the local and state level. After five years of marriage, which eventually included home ownership, I came along in September of 1963. Somewhere along the way, Mom's dream switched from politics to motherhood. My first home at 164 Willowbend Road was a Brighton neighborhood filled with starter homes. I have only a few memories of my first home where I lived the first four years of my life. It was painted white, had three bedrooms, and a huge backyard. My third birthday celebration was a pony party with real ponies which came from a nearby farm. A lady from the farm led the children on pony rides around our big backyard. Dad coined the term "Camp Happy Tots" to describe our vast yard where children loved to play.

We were close friends with our next-door neighbors and Mom made friends with other moms walking their baby carriages through the neighborhood. Mom loved being a full-time mom, having left her job early in her pregnancy. Dad continued his successful law practice, having been named a partner in January 1963. We often accompanied him on his many business trips including such destinations as Beverly Hills, California, Miami, Florida, Atlanta, Georgia, and Canada. There were frequent trips to Washington, DC and New York City which always included time with my grandparents. During those early years on Willowbend Road, I attended Indian Glenn Nursery School. I was very shy and always small for my age. I participated in all the activities, but I also did a lot of passive observing of my classmates, taking it all in. I guess I was a thinker from an early age. I can still picture the fun playground at nursery school where we rode toy horses and tricycles. At home, I loved my dollhouse and matchbox cars, dolls, and my outdoor swing set and ride-on toys.

One of the most special memories of my early childhood was our annual summer vacation to the Lighthouse Inn on Cape Cod, a place I have now taken my own children several times. In the late 1960's, it would take two days to travel there. I listened to eight-track tapes during the long car rides and we stopped to see such historic sites as Old Sturbridge Village, Plymouth Rock, and the Mayflower. The Lighthouse Inn was a quintessential Cape Cod resort. We stayed in a simple little cottage overlooking the ocean and ate all our meals in the Main Inn, in the center of which was a working Lighthouse. Long happy days were spent at the pool and on the beach, playing shuffleboard and ping pong. While daytime attire was bathing suits or shorts, dinner in the Main Inn's dining room required summer dresses for the ladies and ties with jackets for the men. After dinner each evening, we enjoyed organized activities such as bingo.

The world was formal back then. We dressed up to go on airplanes or to go downtown, and even to go to the doctor or dentist. Mom loved shopping for party dresses at Sue Handlin's and Forman's for birthday parties and other events, such as the Valley Club and University Club annual Christmas parties. Grandma Bess sent us beautiful dress coats each year from the New York City department stores where she liked to shop.

Brighton bordered the City of Rochester, but we rarely went downtown. Dad worked in one of the few high-rise buildings which made up the small skyline. Every year at Christmas, we went downtown to visit Santa and have our picture taken on his lap. My sister and I took a ride on the seasonal elevated monorail and waved to Mom down below as we traveled the perimeter of Midtown Plaza. In the center of the indoor plaza, we watched the Clock of Nations open at a designated time revealing puppets from different lands. This very special childhood tradition included a walk through "Christmas Around the World" where each scene depicted a different country exhibiting its holiday traditions with small mechanical figures and decorations.

When I was four, we moved to my second and final childhood home. This brick, Tudor style home, at 425 Claybourne Road, was also in Brighton. The houses were a little bigger, and there were many kids to play with. My parents put a lot of time and effort into this house and I remember many boring errands picking out fabric for the couch or the perfect knob for the kitchen cabinets. At age five, I started Kindergarten at Council Rock School and rode the school bus for the first time. I became an avid reader early on and loved the one on one time, reading with my teacher, Miss Strite. The first series I read on my own were the "Betsy" books, the first one was "B is for Betsy" and I read them all. We used colorful wooden rods to learn math concepts and traced our hands to make Thanksgiving turkeys on colorful paper.

My life as an only child changed on March 17, 1970. I was six-and-a-half years old and while walking home from the bus stop, I saw Grandma Bess in front of my house. She had come from Brooklyn to stay with me because the time had come for my sister to be born. Sarah was born that evening and St. Patrick's Day has been special for our non-Irish family ever since that night. It was love at first sight when I met baby Sarah; my dream of having a baby sister had come true! Her early birthdays were always St. Patrick's Day themed. On her first birthday, Sarah wore an adorable white dress with a green shamrock. I still have a little green plastic shamrock pin from that first birthday. We were a family of four living a happy, secure suburban life against a backdrop of turmoil in faraway lands and a changing culture in our own country. My daily life was completely removed from the Vietnam War and the turbulent 1960's.

CHAPTER II

Divorce: The End of Innocence and
Its Impact on the Elementary School Years

In September of 1970, just after my seventh birthday, the innocence of my early childhood was shattered. My sister Sarah was only six months old when our father took our mother to the Thousand Islands in New York State to tell her he no longer wanted to be married to her. I cannot even imagine that car ride home.

In 1970 Rochester, well-respected lawyers and community leaders did not commonly walk out on their wives and young children. I literally have no firsthand memories of this time, but I have been piecing this jigsaw puzzle of my life together through reading my journals, talking with people who knew my parents, and through years of therapy trying to understand the origins of, and contributing factors to, my mid-life eating disorder.

I have no recollection of my parents telling me about the divorce. Mom, somewhat in denial, said at first that Dad was on a long business trip. This explanation was plausible given that he did travel on business frequently. Mom handled the reality of her divorce by behaving as if nothing had happened, believing that she was protecting us from pain. I learned as an adult that she would cry alone late at night.

With no opportunity to talk about the divorce or its impact I became a shy, introverted young girl; no place for tears, sadness or anger; no place for feelings of any kind. Life in suburbia went on. Dad supported us financially, but he neither lived with us nor was a part of our daily lives.

Soon after the divorce, which my father had to obtain by traveling to Mexico, he remarried, this time to a Rochester socialite. They moved to the neighborhood in Brighton that had the largest and most extravagant homes. It turned out he had been having an affair with this woman whom he had met through their involvement on the Board of Planned Parenthood. I had a bedroom in this huge house, yet I do not have memories of time spent there. I distinctly remember, however, that Dad missed my eighth birthday because he was in Europe with his new wife.

Life went on as an elementary school student at Council Rock School. I spent a lot of time with my best friend, who was in my class, and lived around the corner. We had many sleepovers at her house and her parents often welcomed me to join them on their occasional family day trips. We looked forward to watching *The Brady Bunch* and *The Partridge Family* on Friday nights and we played marathon games of Monopoly. We read the entire *Little House on the Prairie* series by Laura Ingalls Wilder.

On my own street, kids of all ages played happily together. We enjoyed kickball games, spud, hide and seek and bike rides. On warm summer nights, after dinner, we would return outside with our ice cream treats. In winter we climbed snowbanks and built forts until our cheeks were red from the cold and we could no longer feel our fingers. Mom made us hot chocolate when we went inside.

Whenever Dad came to take Sarah and me out to dinner or on some other outing, Mom made us wait outside in front of the house so she would not have to see him. He was always late to pick us up. He did come to my second grade play, *The Wizard of Oz* and recorded on a cassette tape my one line "In Emerald City."

I learned as an adult that Dad lived with a lot of guilt for having left our family and this was a contributing factor to the end of his second marriage after only a couple of years. With two divorces, he had to leave Rochester. Though still a successful lawyer, his reputation as an outstanding member of the community was tarnished beyond repair. My first diary entry was at the age of nine, late in 1972:

I feel horrible. I want to spend Christmas with my father. I think he is lonely and he needs me. Daddy is moving to New York City. I don't want him to go to such a big city. I feel awful.

In the years following the divorce, my diary was the only outlet for expressing such sadness. Life went on and the feelings remained suppressed inside. I developed fears and started to show the first signs of anxiety. I slept with the sheets pulled over my head to feel safe, leaving only a small opening to breathe. From a young age I was put in charge of Sarah. Mom slept until almost noon on most weekend mornings, so Sarah and I watched cartoons and played together, and I fed her breakfast. Mom blamed me if Sarah did anything wrong. One time she tipped over the garbage. Mom blamed me and I had to clean it up. Mom would also leave me in charge when she went out to evening meetings, though I never felt comfortable until she got home and would feel worried if she was even a few minutes late.

I hate to babysit because I am always worried something will happen.

Though Mom tried to do everything she could so that we would never feel like we came from a "broken home," she never did anything to help herself cope with the devastating loss of her marriage. She modeled for us living as if there had been no traumatic change, so that is what I learned to do. Mom could be very loving and always made birthdays and Christmas special, but in the years following the divorce she became increasingly more moody, rigid, and controlling. I often felt like I was walking on eggshells and her unfounded anger and screaming at me scared me. She seemed to release her suppressed emotions on me. Meanwhile, Sarah, six years younger, could do no wrong.

If I do any little thing, Mom gets very upset with me, but not with Sarah.... When I was sick, mom was nice to me, but now that I am better, she seems to always be upset with me for no reason. I feel like running away from home.

Mom and Dad would frequently have heated arguments on the phone, usually about money. I would take Sarah up to my room and close the door to protect her from hearing their arguments, but no one protected me. I internalized all feelings, no one cared how I felt.

> *I hate seeing Mom spend money on clothes for me. I hope she has enough money. I'm worried she won't have enough money because whenever Dad calls, they argue about it.*

What was perhaps a generous divorce agreement at the outset, did not include any cost of living increases. Dad expected Mom to get a job, but she always refused believing that as a single mom she needed to be a full-time mom for us. I grew up sensing Mom's stress whenever taxes or monthly bills were due. Mom accumulated substantial credit card debt through the years and eventually had to file bankruptcy. On the contrary, Dad seemed to spend money needlessly and wastefully. My parents exhibited two extremes and I worried there would not be enough money for daily necessities. Fortunately, my loving, doting maternal grandparents often helped Mom financially when she was in desperate need. For instance, they gave her money for a new washing machine when the old one broke.

After a year in New York City, during which I vaguely remember visiting him, in 1973 Dad moved to Chicago to begin a new life even further away from us. There were certainly phone calls and scheduled visits, but there wasn't the technology there is today to stay closely connected. For those scheduled visits, Sarah and I flew as unaccompanied minors starting at the ages of ten and three. Dad often seemed distracted, even during short visits, and he rarely gave us time alone or even his undivided attention.

> *I feel sorry for Dad. He always has so many things on his mind.*

Dad sometimes would work during our visits or have us spend time with families we did not know. "They have kids your age," he would tell us. There also always seemed to be a new girlfriend for us to meet.

> *[New girlfriend] slept over. Now that dad has met [new girlfriend], he doesn't pay much attention to us. Whenever I told a joke, he never laughed, but when she did, he laughed a lot.*

Unsurprisingly, from a young age, I developed "people pleasing" tendencies, common in children who have experienced trauma. My parents were consumed by their own issues and I often felt ignored. I had neither a voice nor an outlet beyond my journal where I could express my feelings and the impact of my parents' actions on me. I was always put in the middle, listening to each of my parents painting a negative image of the other. Mom was always hard on me and her expectations were often unrealistic. Dad always seemed to lecture me and criticize me. My response to both was to internalize the negative feelings and outwardly try to please them and "be perfect" so as to earn their love and approval.

During the elementary school years, I rarely encountered other kids whose parents were divorced. For several summers, I attended Pioneer Day Camp where I could just be a kid. It was a place for good old-fashioned childhood fun. I have many happy memories from those summer camp sessions and recall meeting one girl whose parents were also divorced.

There is a girl at camp named Jan. Her parents are divorced too. She says I'm the only one who really understands her.

At Pioneer Day Camp, I learned to swim, play group games and enjoy sing a longs and arts and crafts in the wooden pavilion. The counselors drove the campers to and from camp in large 1970's station wagons. There was also an afternoon swim and popsicles before heading home. I looked forward to the camp overnight at the end of each two-week session. We were served pizza instead of the usual bologna or peanut butter and jelly sandwiches. I was happy at camp and had many friends and loved the attention received from my favorite counselors. My only negative memory of camp days was coming home during the summer of the Watergate Hearings and President Richard Nixon's resignation. Mom would be glued to the television when we got home and we couldn't interrupt her even though we had been at camp for hours.

Day to day, Mom, Sarah, and I were a family of three. Many aspects of a safe, happy childhood remained after the divorce and I cherish fond memories of school, friends, holiday traditions and even silly rituals which Mom created. We had "bad manners nights" on Wednesdays with the understanding that on all the other nights our manners were perfect. On Wednesdays we could lick our fingers, chew with our mouth open, and put our elbows on the table. I am grateful for many happy childhood memories, yet my parents' acrimonious divorce and its aftermath left me tinged with sadness, and beneath my smile, were fears, anxiety, and multiple layers of unexpressed feelings and emotions. Dad was in the picture, but he was mostly on the outside, and our relationship would not turn the corner until my college years.

———

CHAPTER III

The Private School Years

My parents believed strongly in the value of a private school education, something from which they had both benefitted. Fortunately, their divorce agreement provided that Dad would pay for both our private school and college tuition.

When Council Rock School ended at the conclusion of fourth grade, I insisted on following the public school path to Twelve Corners Middle School with my best friend since second grade. My parents reluctantly supported my decision, but it would be my last year in public school. I do not have many memories from that year. My best friend and I were able to walk home on nice days and sometimes I would save the milk money Mom had given to me and use it instead to buy candy at Neisners on the way home. Another fifth grade memory was pretending I had a question for my English teacher so I could go up to her desk during independent work time and have one on one time. She was kind to me and I craved her positive attention.

By sixth grade, I was ready for the transition to private school. The Allendale Columbia School sat on a beautiful campus in Pittsford, the next town over. Allendale had been a boys' school and Columbia, a girls' school. They merged a few years before I enrolled. My new school featured small classes taught by dedicated and nurturing teachers. We wore uniforms and in the early years, would stand to show respect when another teacher or administrator walked into the classroom. Lunch was served daily, family style in the dining room rather than cafeteria style. Allendale Columbia started in nursery school and went all the way through high school. Sarah was called a "lifer," having attended all 15 years.

There were wonderful school traditions which we looked forward to every year. On the last morning before Christmas vacation began, children in all grades and their parents gathered for the annual Christmas Breakfast. Several musical selections were performed from the Kindergarten to the Upper School Chorus. Then everyone enjoyed glazed donuts in the dining room before saying our goodbyes until school resumed in early January. Many years later this tradition became the Holiday Breakfast to be more inclusive, and to reflect the more diverse student body.

After the Christmas Breakfast, Mom, Sarah, and I would choose our Christmas tree and spend a cozy afternoon decorating it with Christmas music playing on the stereo. Many of the special ornaments, including the angel that sits atop the tree and the paper Santa I made in nursery school, became treasured keepsakes. A few days after we decorated our tree, my grandparents would arrive from Brooklyn to spend Christmas with us. New Year's Eve was usually spent with Dad in Chicago. He would host a big New Year's Day Open House so most of our holiday visit with him would be spent preparing for this big event.

Another memorable Allendale Columbia tradition was the Strawberry Breakfast, on the Friday of Memorial Day weekend in late spring. The school community gathered in the school courtyard. There were maypole dances and crowns of flowers were presented to the senior girls. Fresh strawberries accompanied the glazed donuts in the dining room.

During the middle school years, we attended Dancing School every other Friday evening. The girls wore white gloves and party dresses, and the boys wore ties and jackets. The instructor, Mr. Victor, with his shiny black shoes, taught us traditional dances such as the waltz and the fox trot. We learned how to go through a receiving line properly. By high school, we attended formal dances every few months hosted by the local country clubs.

Though still very shy at age 11, I easily made friends at my new school.

The transition was smooth despite the fact that most of the girls had already been together in this school for several years.

A pivotal event happened in November of that sixth grade year. As Mom, Sarah, and I often did, we travelled to New York City to spend Thanksgiving with my grandparents. We enjoyed the 1974 Macy's Thanksgiving Day Parade and a carriage ride through Central Park. That year we cut our time short in New York City to visit old friends in Washington, DC. While there we had a series of mishaps, but nothing could compare with the tragedy of a plane crashing in bad weather soon after taking off from the Washington, DC airport on the same day we were scheduled to fly back to Rochester. As we boarded our rescheduled flight the next day, with little improvement in the weather, Mom was very nervous. She held our hands and had us say a prayer as the plane took off. I grew up without organized religion, but we said grace before dinner and a prayer at bedtime. This experience in the plane was different and the beginning of my own personal faith in God. This flight home, through the storm, was also probably the beginning of my anxiety about flying, though I continued to fly several times a year for years to come. Our prayers were answered and the plane landed safely on the snowy runway. The next morning, I woke to a note left by Mom on my bedside table.

> Betsy,
>   You showed tremendous maturity, courage and strength of character during our ordeal, especially getting on the plane calmly when you were no doubt terrified inside. With all my love,
>   Mom-Me

From that experience, I learned that prayer was not simply a pre-meal and pre-bedtime ritual, but that I could pray to God any time, especially when feeling anxious. My journals are filled with prayers in times of high anxiety over day to day things.

> I am babysitting tonight. Please dear God get Mom safely to her meeting and safely home early.

This evolved into both feeling guilty for any negative thoughts and into negating any negative thoughts with positive gratitude. Therefore, I never allowed myself to confront the negative feelings.

> *Tonight, I had a good cry about Dad. I think I was just feeling sorry for myself. I'm grateful our lives are so much better than others.*

Any time I wrote in my journal about Mom's moodiness or her yelling at me for no apparent reason, I followed it up with "*I love my life, thank you God.*"

My anxiety was particularly heightened around health and safety and again I used prayer and my relationship with God as a way to cope. I would start to pray for safe travel for a trip two months away and I would pray for good health before routine pediatric visits. When I simply had a cold, I would thank God that it was nothing serious. My anxiety was not diagnosed until I was in my forties, yet my journals reveal that I clearly suffered from significant anxiety as a child. The fact that I always felt guilty for any negative thoughts or feelings and quickly replaced them with prayer is further evidence of the seeds that were planted early on, and contributed to the development of my mid-life eating disorder.

I loved my small classes and caring teachers at Allendale Columbia, and I thrived academically. I quickly figured out that getting good grades was one way to earn positive attention from Mom. If I could make her proud, she would be happy with me.

> *When Mom read my report cards, she cried of happiness, she is so proud of me.*

I craved that positive attention from her.

> *I hope I will do very well on my report cards. I want Mom to be proud of me.*

That first year at Allendale Columbia, I was not only an honors student, but also won both the sixth grade spelling bee and the sixth grade essay contest. It made me happy and proud because Mom was proud of me and thereby happy with me.

During those school years, I always told Sarah that whenever she had a problem or something on her mind, she could come to me. I was the listener, never the one to express what I was feeling to others. I was the protector and the pleaser.

Mom and Dad were arguing on the phone.
I want everyone to be happy.

I grew up in a safe home and was privileged to attend an outstanding school for seven years. But I grew up feeling a need to be perfect and strong. At the time, I thought being strong meant being positive and unemotional.

During my years at Allendale Columbia, making Mom happy and proud mounted into a tremendous amount of academic pressure as I got older. Mom pressured me to excel. I was bright, motivated, and extremely conscientious, but I never felt support if a grade did not meet Mom's expectations. For example, she would respond to a test grade of 95 by asking if I understood what I did wrong instead of simply complimenting the good grade. I felt very down at times and thankfully was able to confide in a couple of caring teachers about all the pressure I felt.

Dad married wife number three during my first year of high school. He came to Rochester to take me to the father-daughter banquet but later said he did not enjoy himself. I simply accepted it. Consequently, the following year, I had to tag along with a friend and her father. He flew in for the day to hear my speech at the ninth grade forum and he taught me to drive when I turned sixteen. He also took me on a southern college tour during spring break of junior year.

Overall, I saw Dad much less during those high school years, partially because I was busier with school and tennis, but more so because when I visited him in Chicago, he would lecture me and criticize me. He would get upset with me if I failed to send him a card for a minor occasion as if it were my fault that he lived 1,000 miles away.

During my Allendale Columbia years, Mom exhibited, or maybe I just noticed, an obsession with cleaning. She kept the house perfect and nothing was ever out of place. We weren't allowed in the living room or the den, especially if she had just vacuumed.

*This morning Mom got very upset with me because she thought I
messed up a lot of rooms she had just cleaned. But we made up.*

Her rigidity, obsession, and need for control also extended to the kitchen.
She controlled what we ate, when we ate, and how much we ate. I never
learned intuitive eating. We were not allowed into the kitchen to help ourselves to a drink or a snack. She even put the cereal in the bowl for us and
poured the milk on it. This persisted throughout all my years at home. The
only exception was weekend mornings when she would sleep until noon and
I made breakfast for my sister and me. When she woke up, I would have to
give her back rubs before she finally got out of bed.

One time, when I had a friend over after school, I pleaded with Mom to
let me get our snack so my friend wouldn't think I was babied. Fortunately,
Mom let me get the pop tarts out for our after school snack.

My private school education provided me with benefits which went far
beyond the classroom. My gratitude to my parents for my education will
last forever. Our teachers cared about their students holistically, not just as
students they saw for one period in the course of a school day. My teachers
knew me, cared about me, and remembered my family and me far beyond
our graduation year. I received nurturing and care in a way that was lacking
at home. I make a point to go back for my reunions every five years, and I
love reconnecting with old friends and faculty, including those who retired
long ago. Even without social media, our treasured teachers would remember
what year we graduated, where we went to college and would inquire about
a sibling by name. I was a part of something special at my school and it will
always be a special part of me.

Though my report cards routinely exhibited excellent grades, my teachers' comments often read "I wish Betsy would participate more in class dis-
cussions." Even in small classes at a school I loved, I had no voice at this stage
in my life. I developed a fear of failure as a result of Mom's expectations of
perfection. My inability to take risks prevented me from voicing an opinion.
I had a fear of being wrong. In striving to meet Mom's unattainable expectations of perfection, there was no place for questioning her ways or expressing
emotions. She was proud of me when I brought home good grades. I just
went along being a good girl and doing what was expected of me to the best

of my ability. Fear of failure fueled my undiagnosed anxiety and prevented me from being a risk taker. I felt a need to feel in control at all times.

I'm scared to be wrong. This has to do with all my classes and my lack of participation. I never express my feelings out loud. I tend to just accept everything as it is.

I continued to reveal anxiety through prayers in my journals. As well, I expressed guilt whenever I acknowledged I was feeling a little depressed. I thought being a good person meant always being positive, appreciating the good, and never expressing the bad. Aside from confiding in a few caring teachers when I was feeling down or overwhelmed, my journal remained the only safe place I could confide my feelings.

Sometimes lately there is so much inside me that I want to scream or hit something.

I countered any expression of negative feelings in my journal with "I love my life" and I asked God for forgiveness any time I felt sorry for myself.

We didn't do anything exciting today except live. Mom was in a bad mood, but I didn't do anything. I have many things to tell Mom about my feelings and our everyday family life, but I don't know how to say them. Anyway, I am so grateful for everything.

To others Mom was smart, reserved, and always impeccably dressed. Sarah and I felt loved and safe at home and were happy to attend school every day. However, Mom's moodiness and controlling ways became progressively harder to cope with. I became an expert at internalizing difficult emotions because I didn't feel comfortable expressing them, even in my journal. The need to be positive, and to avoid the guilt for feeling anything negative, caused me to suppress all other feelings.

I found peace in walking alone, something that continues to this day.

I love to just walk down the street to the bus stop by myself in the early morning. It makes me feel happy.

By senior year, my class of 45 students came together to savor all those high school "lasts." I had my driver's license by then so Mom would let me have the car if she planned to stay at home cleaning. This was a time of college applications as well as excitement for the future and apprehension about leaving the familiar behind.

Next year we will all be starting over, new friends and new places. It's kind of scary when I think about it. I look forward to college and I think it will be good for me.

I was excited when accepted to Brown University and Mom "cried from happiness."

Every time I think about what a happy day it was for me, I think about how sad a day it was for others.

Graduation in June 1981 was a beautiful occasion. We wore long white dresses and the boys wore blue blazers along with the traditional school tie. Mom, Sarah, my grandparents, and Dad and his third wife were there to celebrate this milestone with me. I cherish the memories of caring teachers who in some ways understood me better than I understood myself. School was a place where I felt happy and safe, and where, as a quiet member of my class, I was respected for my academic and tennis accomplishments.

My tennis career, which will be explored in the next chapter, began early in my private school years, providing a safe outlet and a source for developing self-esteem.

CHAPTER IV

——

Tennis

Mom loved the sport of tennis. I don't know if she played as a child, but as an adult she was an average player at best. She was introduced to the sport in the 1940s by her Uncle Vic, who had served as a Chair Umpire at Wimbledon. During several summers in the 1950s, Mom served as a linesperson, traveling the Eastern Seaboard to tournaments featuring the best amateur players in the world. This was before the Open Era of Professional tennis which did not begin until 1968. Mom was not only on court calling the lines during matches, but she was also socializing with the players at each tour stop. Players such as Maureen Connelly and Ken Rosewall, who were top players in the world at that time, have since been inducted into the International Tennis Hall of Fame.

I started taking weekly tennis lessons at Mid-Town Tennis Club when I was 10 years old. This was during the tennis boom of the 1970s and the indoor club where I took lessons had 16 courts which were almost always busy. The lessons were okay, but I did not show much potential at that time. Mom liked to watch professional tennis on television, and I would often join her. She would remark that some of these tournaments were played at historic clubs where she had officiated 20 years earlier.

For my 11th birthday, in late summer 1974, Mom planned a trip for us to attend the US Open at Forest Hills. This special trip started with a birthday dinner at the Plaza Hotel with my grandparents. Afterwards, they took Sarah home with them to Brooklyn Heights and Mom and I checked into the Manhattan hotel where most of the players were staying. At the hotel we were excited to hang out in the lobby each evening watching the players coming and going. For three days we watched professional tennis at the magnificent West Side Tennis Club in Forest Hills, New York. I loved waiting by the clubhouse to get autographs from famous players I had seen on television. These players included Jimmy Connors, Chris Evert, and my favorite, Stan Smith, all of whom became legends of the game. This was the 1970s and I was enamored by the cute tanned male players with long flowing hair and wearing beaded chokers around their necks. This time alone with Mom, away from home, was very special and after this amazing trip my passion for tennis was born.

I love tennis. I want to be a Forest Hills Champ.

We repeated this special birthday trip for the next two years. I started to take my tennis more seriously, trying my best in my weekly clinics. This coincided with the beginning of my private school years. While in my journals, I expressed my love for school and tennis, I also began writing down what I ate for dinner each night.

My body is changing a lot. I'm going on a little diet.

I have no independent recollection as to why I wrote that journal entry. There was no eating disorder, yet the seeds were being subtly planted as my journals revealed an increasing focus on food and body image.

During the summer of 1975 when I was 11 going on 12, tennis became more important to me. I played every day that summer at the Valley Club, the same club where our summers at the pool began each year with the Memorial Day Parade. I worked on my tennis skills with the Club's Head Professional in both private and group lessons. I played regularly with Mom and other adult women players at the club.

I think I have a good chance of being a great tennis player some day.

This was my first summer not at Pioneer Day Camp and my last summer before tennis really took over. In addition to playing tennis regularly at the Valley Club, I also spent time at the pool each summer day, swimming and chatting with friends after tennis. At home, I enjoyed time with friends and playing outside with the neighborhood kids.

At the last clinic of the summer, we competed in a little tournament.

I couldn't believe it, I won! I got a can of tennis balls and a sweatband. I was so happy.

By now, I was old enough to stay at the club without Mom and spent many happy days there during the summer of 1975. I loved the independence at both the courts and the pool.

Mom and Sarah went home because Mom had to clean the house.

One day towards the end of that transitional summer, a woman at the club complimented me for my tennis ability.

A lady told me I play very well. I am so flattered, and I love to be noticed for my tennis. I hope to be a famous champion some day.

Though that summer was only the infancy of my tennis career, it marked the beginning of chasing my dreams, working hard on something important to me, and most crucially, developing self-esteem. Tennis helped me to feel good about myself, especially when I received positive attention from others as I improved and reaped the benefits of my effort and dedication.

By the following summer in 1976, my tennis had reached a new level. I had been taking weekly private lessons with one of the top coaches in Rochester and I played in my first Eastern Tennis Association sanctioned tournament where I won my first match before losing to a highly ranked player.

My journal entries, meanwhile, continued to reveal the anxiety I felt around health and safety and the frequent prayers that had become a coping mechanism. Mom remained moody and obsessed with cleaning behaviors.

Mom was mad at me because I didn't hear her when she called me in to dinner. We sure ate quietly tonight.

I continued to worry when Mom spent money on me, fearing she wouldn't have enough for other expenses, and that it would lead to heated arguments with Dad. But I now also had tennis as a healthy outlet for my anxiety.

I continued to love school. I studied hard and made Mom proud when I brought home good grades. Now I shared her love for tennis as well. I had not yet surpassed her level, so we continued to play frequently at the Valley Club. We would often pretend that the set we played was the final set for the Wimbledon Championship. Tennis made me feel good about myself, brought me a positive connection with Mom, and provided a healthy physical outlet for my emotions.

At the Valley Club I am known for my tennis. I love it.

That summer of 1976, the nation's bicentennial, I was 12 ½ and was invited to try out for the Excellence Group at the Tennis Club of Rochester. Another of the top coaches in the area ran this elite summer clinic for top junior players in the area. The Tennis Club of Rochester (TCR), about a 20-minute drive from my home, had 24 courts, a basic clubhouse, a snack bar, and a pool. I was excited to be chosen for the Excellence Program and Mom, who had anxiety about the speed of highway driving, was thrilled that we could carpool with the family of another tennis player from Brighton who was in the same group. The clinics were filled with challenging drills, and after each session we ran two miles. I was one of the youngest players, and one of the weakest players, that summer.

I had my first excellence group. I like it. I'm proud to be in the highest level of lessons for juniors. I hope [coach] will never think I am not good enough.

TCR would become my summer home away from home for years to come. There were no signs of my anxiety when I was at TCR doing what I loved to do. I played tennis for several hours every weekday, going home in the late afternoon. In addition to the clinics, there were practice matches and just hitting the ball with other junior players. To reserve a court, we placed our laminated photo identification cards into slots on the large wooden court sign in board. It was an honor to be one of the select group of juniors who could not be "bumped" by adult players when our junior ID cards had reserved a court.

Off court, many of the junior players, both boys and girls, hung out together in the clubhouse lounge. We talked about any topic that came to mind. We played backgammon, ate lunch, and flirted innocently. My best tennis friend and I talked to each other about which boys we thought were cute.

That summer of 1976 I started playing tournaments more regularly including my first out of town tournament, about one and a half hours away, in Syracuse, New York. Sedgewick Farm Racquet Club hosted the Central New York Junior Championships every July and the event always seemed to be held during the hottest week of the summer. An old club house overlooked the red clay courts and players were required to wear all white clothing.

It was very professional looking and crowded. Kids were walking around in warmups with two or three rackets.

I won my first match in this, my first out of town tournament, before losing in the next round to a top seeded player. The experience made me want to work harder both on and off the court so I could advance further in tournaments. I wrote in my journal after a full day of tennis at TCR.

When I came home, I gave myself a good work out. I ran around the block at full speed without stopping and did sit ups, jump-roping and jumping jacks.

A highlight of that summer was winning my first trophy when my partner and I were finalists in the TCR 14 and Under Doubles Club Championships.

It was like a professional match.

And after the end of the summer awards ceremony.

I felt proud going up to get my large trophy.

During my pre-teen years, Sarah and I continued to travel to Chicago to visit Dad and whomever he was dating at the time.

Please God, guide our plane safely to Chicago, I hope we deserve it.

My passion for tennis went beyond the court. I not only loved to play tennis, but I was also a huge fan. I enjoyed watching tennis on TV with Mom and I read *World Tennis* magazine cover to cover when it arrived in the mail each month. I would cut out pictures of my favorite players, including Bjorn Borg and Stan Smith, and tape them on my bedroom wall right next to my bed. Tennis gave me a sense of purpose. I learned how to set goals and work to achieve them. I learned to both win and lose with grace.

That fall of 1976, I entered eighth grade. I practiced several days a week at Mid-Town Tennis Club, including private lessons, clinics, and practice matches against new tennis friends I had met during the summer at TCR.

I played many more Eastern Tennis Association sanctioned tournaments in nearby Upstate New York cities such as Buffalo and Syracuse. I often went with my best tennis friend and her dad because Mom would not drive on the highway and she had Sarah to care for at home. Mom insisted that I find a pay phone, wherever I was, to call her with my results immediately after each match. I had the best feeling when reporting a win but reporting a loss felt as if I were letting Mom down. She was generally supportive, but I sensed when she was disappointed.

The tennis club was a place where I had a healthy physical outlet, felt good about myself, and received positive attention from adults. My tennis was a positive way to cope with what was missing at home. Having a physical outlet by hitting tennis balls helped to alleviate the emotions I was so good at internalizing. This physical outlet reduced anxiety and my tennis success continued to fuel my self-esteem and self-confidence. At the club, there were many young 20-something male teaching pros and, during off court time, I loved engaging in conversations with whomever was around. The more success I had with my tennis, the more positive attention I received.

The pros at Mid-Town are so nice to me. I like the attention.

Two momentous events at this stage of my tennis career occurred the following summer when I was 13 ½. At TCR, I won the 14 and Under Singles Club Championships, beating two of my biggest rivals in back to back matches. Mom said I would always remember that first singles tournament win. I was excited to add this meaningful trophy to my trophy shelf in my bedroom; I had designated this special shelf after winning the tennis ball can at the clinic tournament.

I was so proud of myself.

I knew Mom was proud of me too, though nothing at home had changed.

Sarah and I played together all morning while Mom cleaned.

That summer, I also reached the final for the first time in an Eastern Tennis Association sanctioned tournament. Unfortunately, on the morning of the final, I awoke with a fever and a bad sore throat. I didn't tell Mom because I wanted to play the match. I played and lost. By the time I got home, my fever had risen to 103 degrees. Catching a summer virus when I had such a great opportunity was bad timing. Mom was especially nice to me when I was sick and commiserated with me at the misfortune of being sick for the big final.

Mom and I *"cried with joy"* when I learned that October that I had earned my first Eastern tennis ranking, #34 among 14 and under girls in all of New York State, including New York City, Long Island, and Northern New Jersey.

I will always be grateful to Mom for allowing and encouraging me to follow my tennis dreams. The pressure on me was subtle, but it was there. Mom loved the attention she received from my success and she seemed to live through me as a tennis mom of one of the top local juniors. I still felt guilty when she spent money on me, even when it was supporting my tennis passion.

I got new tennis shoes. They weren't on sale. I feel guilty for Mom spending so much money on me.

Though Dad seemed somewhat jealous of my tennis as it brought me closer to Mom, he did pay for my private lessons, my TCR membership and some of my travel expenses. He had a hard time when I surpassed his level on the court, which I did early on, as he was not a strong player. He would come and meet me at tournaments from time to time, but our relationship was becoming more strained during my high school years, as he accused me of prioritizing tennis over him.

Dad says I think too much about myself and not enough about him. I started crying. I was upset but just went along with what he was saying, although I wanted to argue. I was upset and cried myself to sleep. Tomorrow I will get it all out on the court.

During my high school years, my tennis improved significantly. I achieved higher Eastern rankings and began to travel further to tournaments several times a year. The biggest Eastern tournaments were held on Long Island. By the age of 14, I was thrilled to be sponsored by Wilson Sporting Goods. I received free Chris Evert Autograph rackets, tennis shoes, t-shirts and even a large travel bag.

Thankfully, I will never know how my high school years would have unfolded had I not had tennis to help me to feel good about myself and to use as an outlet for my otherwise unexpressed emotions.

A turning point in my tennis career came when I was 15. Until that time, I had done well in many tournaments and had brought home many trophies, but I routinely beat the players I was supposed to beat and lost to players ranked above me. At this particular New York tournament, I played one of the highest ranked players in New York. I lost the first set but kept fighting and came back to win the second set. Although I lost the third set and thus the match, I learned an important lesson that day. By taking a set from a top player, I learned that I belonged on that court and that if I focused on the tennis ball rather than on who was on the other side of the net, anything was possible. My self-belief grew tremendously. Any time I stepped foot on the court, going forward, I had a deep-down belief that I was capable of winning.

During my high school years, tennis was more important to me than social life. I had good friends in school and attended dances and sporting events throughout high school, but I spent many Saturday nights home watching TV and playing scrabble with Mom. It was my choice to miss many parties and social gatherings. I never had a fake ID to try to get into bars. I neither drank nor smoked as many of my classmates did. I spent many weekends away at tournaments or stayed home because I was practicing early the next morning. My school friends and classmates respected me for my tennis, specifically for my dedication to something that was very important to me.

I played on my high school girls' team for three years and have many fond memories from that time. I viewed high school tennis as an "extra," outside the sanctioned tournament circuit which was all about rankings. High School tennis allowed me to be part of a team and represent my school. I loved it when my favorite teachers would show up courtside to watch my matches and I enjoyed the positive attention at school the next day after my match wins. I was able to win sectional championships each year and compete in the New York State High School Championships. In my final year, I advanced to the quarterfinals, the final eight in the state. I lost to the eventual winner who incidentally went on to compete successfully at Wimbledon. I proudly wore my sectional patches on my high school corduroy tennis jacket.

In the fall of my senior year, I was invited to represent the Eastern Tennis Association in the 18 and under USTA National Indoor Championships in Plainville, Massachusetts. Each section of the USTA could send a specific number of players to Nationals. I had played in big tournaments before, but nothing like this.

I saw girls I have only heard and read about. This tournament is the big time of Junior Tennis.

I travelled with a tennis friend from Buffalo. We were met at the airport by a tournament representative and we received housing with local families.

I feel so happy and independent and I'm so grateful for safe traveling.

Though I lost in the first round, it was an amazing experience playing in a tournament of this magnitude. I loved traveling independently and staying with a friendly and welcoming family. I was excited to play in the same tournament with many players who would go on to have successful professional careers.

I was hitting the ball so well like I definitely belong in a national tournament.

One of the highlights at my first nationals occurred when I met the Head Coach of Brown University from nearby Providence, Rhode Island. He was interested in talking with me and watching me play. The college recruiting process had begun. The Brown Coach followed up with letters and phone calls over the next several months, and I was increasingly excited about the possibility of playing college tennis in the Ivy League.

Everything has been working out so perfectly that I'm scared something is going to go wrong.

Upon returning home, I was happy to be back in school and loved being asked about my experience.

In my journals, I noted my height and weight from time to time in addition to nightly recounting of what I ate for dinner. Over the holidays, a month after my trip to Nationals, I wrote in my journal that I felt like I needed to go on a diet after eating so many restaurant meals. I have no independent recollection of negative feelings about food or body image.

An article about me in the newspaper a few months later mentioned my height and weight. I was tiny and have no idea why at that time I would write such things in my journals. The focus of the newspaper article was about playing on the boys' tennis team during the spring of my senior year. *She's Beating the Boys*, the headline read, and went on to explain how despite my small frame I was able to beat many high school boys who were obviously bigger and stronger. This was another validating experience, another enjoyable adjunct to my tennis career. The boys were kind and respectful towards me, and they welcomed me as a teammate without resentment. The coach would joke that when I beat a boy from another team, he would face a long bus ride home after losing to a girl.

In May of senior year, 1981, as the end of high school was drawing near, I travelled to Long Island, New York, for the biggest Eastern Tennis Association Tournament of the year. In what was the culmination of my junior tennis career, I dug deep, used that self-belief, and beat several players ranked well above me. With those wins, I earned a spot in all three of the USTA National 18 and under Championships to be held that summer in San Francisco, California, Memphis, Tennessee, and Hartford, Connecticut. It was a summer of traveling independently, amazing tennis, and new friendships with girls from all over the country. I received positive attention in the Rochester tennis community during my summer of travel around the country. Of course, Mom loved the attention she received because of my tennis success and I felt good that she was proud of me.

The summer of 1981, my junior tennis career came to an exciting end and with it came my highest Eastern ranking and my first USTA National Girls 18 and under ranking.

> *Because of tennis I am independent and very self-disciplined. I also have gained self-confidence. Through tennis I have travelled and met kids from other cities. I have enjoyed every minute of the last five years and will never regret the sacrifices. I wouldn't trade my life with anyone.*

My tennis coach since the age of 12 was a Brown Alumnus who had played tennis and squash there during the late 1960s. He was thrilled I would be attending his alma mater and stopped by my house with a bottle of champagne and his large Brown University mug for me to keep.

Though we both left Rochester many years ago, we have maintained contact. He has come to Providence occasionally to visit our alma mater and in 2019, when he attended a milestone reunion, he made time to watch me coach a high school state championship semi-final match. I enjoyed introducing my childhood coach to many people in my present adult tennis life. I always looked up to him. He had high standards and did not give compliments freely so when he said something positive about my tennis, it was especially meaningful.

He was interviewed for the newspaper article about my playing on the boys' team my senior year:

Clearly, she's the best because she's worked the hardest. She has a powerful hit from the baseline, and she keeps her cool head and maturity on the court, which is very hard to beat.

I was ready for the next chapter of my tennis career, Division One College Tennis at Brown University.

CHAPTER V

—

The College Years

The summer of 1981, when I was 17 ½ years old, was highlighted not only by my traveling independently to three National tennis tournaments, but also by my first significant boyfriend. We had known each other for several summers at Tennis Club of Rochester but did not start dating until that summer following my high school graduation. He had his own car and liked to take me to dinner at nice restaurants. We also saw movies and played miniature golf. I spent many more nights out that summer, which was normal for a 17-year-old, but for Mom this meant less time with her. She would give me the silent treatment and be generally cool towards me. Mom would remind me how often I was out rather than home with her.

I feel badly that I was out so many nights this week. I wish Mom didn't make me feel guilty.

Looking back, I'm sure she was having a hard time with the fact that I would soon be leaving for college. She accepted that I would be nearly 400 miles from home because I would be attending Brown University and playing Division One college tennis. Sarah would be home for many more years, but she was so young. Mom considered me her best friend and I was the closest she had to having an adult at home with her. As for me, I have only good memories from the summer of 1981.

I'm really happy right now. I'm really looking forward to going to Brown. I still have to be more independent though.

September was marked by my 18th birthday and packing, not only for college, but for a move from the house that had been my home since the age of four. Mom had decided several months earlier to sell the house and rent a townhouse in a complex in another part of Brighton. She gave me the old sheets and towels to bring to college so I would have "reminders from home." Meanwhile, she selected all new accessories for the townhouse.

Since Mom didn't drive on the highway, our close family friend offered us not only her station wagon, but also her driving and wonderful company for the trip to Providence. Sarah stayed with a friend, we packed the car, and off we went. In the back of the station wagon was my black trunk, a few suitcases, and the new electric typewriter I had received as a high school graduation gift. Our family friend took charge of the trip and the move into my freshman dorm. Together with Mom, she helped me settle in before leaving for the long drive back to Rochester.

I sat on the floor in a circle with my freshman unit on my first night at college. Our Resident Counselor, an upper-class student, began our full week of orientation with ice breakers and "get to know you" games. My roommate and I got off to a good start and ate many meals together the first few weeks.

Brown took me out of my comfort zone which was the best thing that could have happened to me. This mid-size university far from home was liberal and diverse, with students from every state in the US and from around the world.

I was somewhat independent from traveling for tennis, but college gave me a new kind of independence and freedom. Though away at college, I still craved Mom's approval. Despite the issues with her at home, I felt close to her. Early on in my college experience, I remained very much in Mom's realm of control. A few years would pass before I was ready for and capable of freedom.

I was still very shy and had my serious boyfriend from home several hours away at another college. All I really knew were academics and tennis, so I didn't jump into the new college social life that was there for me. I had several acquaintances that first year, but I needed time to develop real friendships.

The first few weeks at Brown I used a paper map to find my classes. This was long before cell phones and "map apps." I made my first friend on the walk to the tennis courts for our first tennis practice. She was the top recruit from our strong group of freshmen. As we walked to that first practice, we found out that we both had parents who had divorced when we were young girls. She remains a close friend to this day.

The tennis team provided me with connection in a small group within a big university. The team spent a lot of time together and I earned a starting position on the team in my first semester. Our Ivy League season was in the Spring, but we played several non-league matches in the Fall and practiced year-round. Mom still expected me to call her after every match and she wanted to make sure I was playing enough tennis. She went as far as strongly urging me to call a local club to find a strong player for additional practice. Of course, I followed Mom's wishes despite having outstanding practice with my young team comprised of the biggest and strongest recruiting class in Brown women's tennis history. I remained under Mom's control 400 miles from home.

Mom came to visit me for Parents Weekend about a month into my fresh-man year. I loved showing her around the campus and we shopped together for a winter coat and a comforter for my bed. Dad, who was not involved in my move to Brown or Parents Weekend, visited soon after Mom's visit. He rented a car so we could explore more of the area including beautiful New-port, Rhode Island, less than an hour from campus.

My other visitor that first semester was my boyfriend. We had written each other letters and talked to each other on the phone since saying good-bye at the end of the summer. We spent a happy weekend together. I visited him on another weekend, taking two buses to get there.

Mom's OCD manifested itself in her insisting on writing a daily letter to me, even when she didn't have much to say. She claimed she wanted my mailbox to be full. In those days there were neither emails nor a quick text as a way to communicate. Phone calls were limited to about once a week and long-distance calls were always after 5:00 p.m. when the rates went down. The exception, of course, was calling "collect" with my results after a tennis match.

After two months of adjusting to college life, I was feeling homesick by early November, counting the days until I would go home for Thanksgiving. I had been navigating college classes for the first time and as a conscientious student, spent so much of the time studying when not on the tennis court or traveling to matches at other colleges. I had my tennis teammates and many acquaintances, but I had yet to experience so much of what Brown offered outside the classroom.

In a letter to Mom during this period of homesickness, I expressed guilt for my feelings.

> *When I get upset like that, I feel guilty because there are so many people with awful problems and I can't even identify what it is that causes me to cry.*

Later in the same letter, I reassured Mom that I was okay.

> *I want you to know I am in total control of myself and that my periods of depression and thinking too much are not continuous.*

In college, the freedom around food was wonderful. For the first time in my life, I could eat what I wanted, when I wanted and could decide how much to eat. At first, I ate very freely in the "all you can eat" dining halls, including delicious desserts without any guilt attached. Then by early November, coincidentally around the time of my bout with homesickness, I started eating very little at each meal. This was my first experience of restricting. Although I still played a lot of tennis and was aware that I needed energy, I ate very small meals and no desserts. Perhaps I felt out of control after sudden freedom with food or maybe this was my way of coping with feeling homesick. For some unknown reason, there is no journal from that year to provide clues, but it was my first independent recollection of using food as an unhealthy coping mechanism. Fortunately, an eating disorder did not take hold at that time.

By the time I went home for Thanksgiving, I was ready for mom's home cooked meals and I had no choice but to live and eat under her control. I was happy to be home, but the new townhouse was very unfamiliar to me. My bedroom was a fraction of the size and Mom had either discarded or given away many of my childhood belongings. While home for Thanksgiving I tried to avoid upsetting Mom by balancing the time spent with Mom and Sarah, with time with my boyfriend.

When I returned to Brown after Thanksgiving, I wrote Mom a letter in which I actually apologized for spending time with my boyfriend.

> *Please, please, please forgive me for being so thoughtless concerning the time I spent with [my boyfriend] and not with you. I love you so much and want more than anything for you to be happy.*

I always told Mom what she wanted to hear. My letters to her often reflected mundane facts from my life at college, including how much tennis I played, how much studying I did, and even what I ate for dinner. I would reassure her how much I missed her and wanted to be home.

A highlight of second semester was the spring break tennis team trip to Virginia. We traveled by van to compete against several strong schools in that area. This new experience was great for team bonding. April brought my first Ivy League season and I was happy to be in the starting line-up for every single match. By May, I was ready to get through my final exams and return home for the summer.

That summer of 1982 was as if I had never left. I played a lot of tennis, chauffeured Mom and Sarah to Sarah's tournaments, and spent time at home and out with my boyfriend. I was proud of myself for making it through my first year of college. After a year of independence, I still had no voice or freedom at home, but there was something comforting about returning to the security and predictability of life in Rochester.

Shortly, after my 19th birthday, I returned to Brown in the fall of 1982 for my sophomore year. I was more confident and comfortable than the previous year. I had a successful fall tennis season playing higher in the line-up and by now had developed several close friendships. Although more enmeshed in life at Brown, I remained aware of Mom's control and still craved her approval. I needed her to be happy with me. Sophomore year brought the end of my relationship with my boyfriend. Maintaining a long-distance relationship was difficult and even when we were home, he felt he was third in line for my time and attention behind my family and tennis. Without that relationship, I became more engaged in social life at Brown.

When I returned home for winter break, Mom revealed over lunch that she had recently been diagnosed with breast cancer and was scheduled for a mastectomy two days before Christmas. Such a scary, difficult diagnosis, yet I have no memories of significant conversations with her expressing either of our emotions or fears. She insisted that we open our presents before she went into the hospital. My grandparents arrived to spend Christmas with us as they always did, and we learned Mom had not yet told her parents about her diagnosis and scheduled surgery. We visited Mom in the hospital and had a quiet Christmas dinner at the home of the same family friend who had taken me to Brown freshman year. Mom had charged her with telling my grandparents the news upon their arrival in Rochester.

Once Mom recovered from her surgery, there was no further treatment and we went on with our lives. I would learn many years later that her doctor had recommended chemotherapy because of two positive lymph nodes, but she had declined without any discussion.

In the years that followed, we rarely talked about her being a breast cancer survivor. At one point, she announced she was going on a no fat diet to make sure her cancer never returned. I learned from her that somehow eating fat must be bad.

Spring break of sophomore year marked the first of three consecutive years of tennis team trips to Southern California. I was anxious on the long plane rides, but thoroughly enjoyed the sunshine, highly competitive tennis, and the camaraderie with my teammates.

I went home the summer of 1983 and spent a lot of time with Mom and Sarah. Mom still did not drive on the highway, so I was the designated chauffer for all Sarah's tennis trips which were more frequent and often further away as she became a better player. I also worked on my own tennis and taught tennis lessons to local children and adults. I started dating another Rochester guy and once again had to contend with guilty feelings whenever Mom made me feel I wasn't spending enough time with her. She never outright said anything specifically, but her moods let me know.

By my junior year, I was slowly trying to break out of the tight web Mom had spun around me. Brown opened my mind to the wider world and allowed the time and space to think about life beyond Mom's relentless control. My tennis identity remained very important to me and was a tremendous source of self-esteem. I now had a healthy balance in my college life. In addition to being a conscientious psychology major and a dedicated college tennis player, I had many good friends and an enjoyable and active social life. I still felt close to Mom and we spent a fun Parents Weekend in Boston that year. She continued to send daily letters but was increasingly absorbed in Sarah's tennis life and less interested in mine. Now at the age of 20 and comfortable with my life at Brown, I was finding it hard to fathom another summer at home without the freedom and independence I had become accustomed to in college.

Though I was maturing and exhibiting personal growth, it was not without struggle, especially a strong need to be in control. Junior year I started keeping a detailed journal once again.

I feel so good when I have everything under control. It's easy to get depressed when things aren't under control.

There were also multiple instances of a heightened focus on food and body image, though no full-blown eating disorder. I wrote in my journal after eating a peanut butter cookie

I hate my eating habits. I want to eat less and feel thin.

After eating cereal and a bagel for breakfast, I allowed myself only an apple for lunch. My journal revealed that I did this on many days. I do not have an independent recollection of issues with food and body image at this time, though clearly something was brewing. I remember thinking that certain tennis outfits made me feel thin and I liked that feeling. My journal also reveals the day following eating a lot while out for a friend's birthday.

I'm falling into my trap again about weight loss. Tomorrow I'll have to go back on my diet.

And then a few weeks later:

> *I gained 5 pounds over vacation. I need will power and self-discipline to lose weight. Help!*

These journal entries are clearly evidence that I had excessive thoughts about food and body image, yet I have no independent recollection of this focus.

My letters to Mom during my college years revealed issues with food and body image.

> *I had ice cream at Baskin Robbins which I rationalized by my needing change for laundry.*
> *Today I wore that yellow shirt that I always said makes me look fat.*

I also remarked in another letter:

> *I actually felt full after dinner; that doesn't happen very often.*

I continued to feel guilty about spending money.

> *I did something I never do. I bought myself a pair of $5.00 stylish dangly earrings. I love them, but I shouldn't have spent money on myself.*

Emotionally at this time, I was torn between not wanting to upset Mom yet yearning to be more independent. Over the long holiday break, I started hinting to Mom about the possibility of getting a non-tennis job the following summer. She made it clear that she disapproved. When I returned to school, I wrote Mom a letter about some of my "growing up" issues. Her letter in response was not supportive at all and its emotional toll on me clearly played out with food.

> *I've got to lose 5 pounds. I'll be happier then.*

I felt the need to loosen Mom's grip, yet I loved her and always felt close to her.

> *I called Mom just to say I love you. She gets depressed a lot these days and I have a lot to do with it. I am getting older and growing up. I hate to have Mom be upset. All I want is for her to be happy. It's kind of scary for me during this transitional time in my life. I must keep things from happening too fast.*

My relationship with Dad remained difficult, but soon would be changing.

> *Dad and I argued on the phone. He makes me so mad.*

About a month later, early on in second semester of junior year, Dad and I had a very encouraging conversation.

> *I had a good talk with Dad. I raised the possibility of working this summer in a city such as Washington. I don't know how I would tell Mom. It would be so good for me to be on my own, but I also love being at home. Dad liked my idea.*

I also expressed in my journal at this time that I was glad my Valentine's Day package from Mom did not include chocolates or candy. In a letter pertaining to another Valentine's Day, I wrote:

> *Thanks for the chocolates. They will make me fat, but I will eat them.*

In late February 1984, Dad came to visit me at Brown. It was the first time we had spent an entire weekend together without him lecturing me or criticizing me. Instead, he was excited to help me execute my idea of living and working in a city that summer. He had been waiting a long time for me to express any desire for independence and he had the resources and connections to make it happen. During the next few weeks, I was overwhelmed by the excitement and apprehension about the summer and wracked with uncertainty about how I would tell Mom.

My head is so cluttered. I'm 99% sure I'm going to DC this summer. How do I tell Mom? Help! I think too much. I wish I could relax.

On our tennis team spring break trip to California, I could finally focus on being a college tennis player and less on being in the middle between Mom and Dad and my own conflicting emotions. In California, we played matches against west coast schools, practiced in the warm sunshine, and enjoyed days off at the beach, shopping, and Disneyland.

I felt so happy all day and thin too. It's so easy to just be happy here. I love tennis trips.

In the first 20 years of my life, the most difficult thing I did was tell Mom I would not be spending the summer at home.

I'm so scared everything is going to explode when I get home. I feel guilty, I've never openly disagreed with Mom.

She could not be happy for me which was hard because I still wanted and needed her approval. It was all about her. She was hurt, devastated, and sad, and the fact that Dad was making it all possible made it worse. Once home after my final exams, there was much tension between Mom and me. She accused me of changing so much and putting everyone ahead of her.

I cried myself to sleep.

Dad came to Rochester in early June 1984 to drive with me to Washington, DC. My fortune on a Bazooka Bubble Gum wrapper read "Don't fear change, it's for the best." In Washington, Dad helped me settle into the apartment that he had found for me to sublet and helped me to figure out the Metro, the subway, which I would take to and from work each day. My job was in a law firm where I would be helping out wherever I was needed. Dad knew many lawyers at the firm. He still lived in Chicago but travelled to DC often for his work, so we had time together. Dad had made all the arrangements for this life changing summer and we were both excited. Leaving Rochester, however, was not easy.

It was so sad saying goodbye to Mom and Sarah. I'm so full of mixed emotions. I cried in the car behind my sunglasses.

During this pivotal summer of 1984, I experienced independence on an unprecedented level, was making decisions for myself, and was learning how to stand on my own two feet. I was learning about life outside mom's bubble and I liked it.

I feel very comfortable here. I am enjoying the independence.

I worked in the office all day and played tennis many evenings. I even won a big tennis tournament in DC. The best part of that memorable summer though was spending time with Dad and developing a relationship for the first time. I loved picking him up at the airport, having dinner with him and sharing the details of my DC life that he had made possible.

After many wonderful weekends with Dad during that summer of 1984, he wrote me a letter that still brings tears to my eyes.

Oh, it is such a treat getting to know you. I love you and appreciate you dearly. Don't ever change.

At the age of 20, I finally heard the words I had been waiting to hear since my parents' divorce. This was the first time Dad had expressed appreciation for who I was.

I loved time alone in my apartment, experimented with cooking, and enjoyed a fun social life.

It was fun going out on the town even on a work night. I'm so happy here in Washington. I hope all continues to go well.

In my journal, I expressed my changed feelings toward Dad.

I met up with Dad. I love him. I cooked dinner for him for the first time. I'm so proud of myself.

I loved the freedom on warm summer evenings in the city. After dinner outside with a friend on a beautiful night, I remarked in my journal:

It was paradise.

During my two months in Washington, I saw Mom and Sarah once when I drove up to New York to spend the weekend with them at one of Sarah's tennis tournaments.

*I ate so much. I want to go on a diet **for real.***

Other than that weekend, I kept in touch with them by phone.

I keep getting the feeling that Mom isn't happy to hear from me when I call her.

However, when I went back home in early August I was greeted with homemade "welcome home" signs. I have no idea what changed her mindset while I was away.

Mom told me how proud she is of me. That meant a lot to hear it from her.

While home, I reflected on my experience that summer in Washington, DC.

This summer I have really gotten a lot of confidence in myself in something other than tennis and schoolwork.

The summer of 1984 came to an end with my 21st birthday celebration in Rochester with Mom, Sarah, and a close friend from high school. And then, off I went to Providence to begin my senior year at Brown.

Senior year in college was unforgettable. I was more relaxed and had a very active social life which included both drinking more and going out with friends more often than in previous years. Ironically, as I enjoyed myself more, my grades and tennis were better than ever.

By this time, when I returned home for vacations, I couldn't wait to return to school.

I was co-captain of the tennis team and a confident leader for the younger players. I was the only one from our original recruited group to play on the team all four years. I was proud that I had played in every single match through every season over the four years. By the spring Ivy League season, I was the number one singles player and half of the top double team. These memories are among my most treasured, especially the special friendships, all the travel, the apex of my tennis career, and life lessons learned.

A few short months after my amazing DC summer and with senior year happily underway, Dad called on a Sunday morning to tell me he had been diagnosed with colon cancer. My first reaction was that this would be like Mom's cancer experience two years earlier. I thought Dad would have surgery to remove the cancer and we would go on with our lives.

It was during first semester final exams, but with Mom's blessing I flew to Chicago to be with Dad at the time of his surgery. He was between marriages at this point and though he had many dear friends and colleagues, he was otherwise alone. I stayed with one of Dad's close friends who sat with me at the hospital while Dad underwent surgery to remove the cancer from his colon.

Dad's first cousin, whom I hadn't seen since before my parents' divorce, was Chief of Gastroenterology at this hospital. He didn't perform the surgery, but he came to talk to me in the surgical waiting area following Dad's surgery. He delivered the devastating news that the cancer had already spread to Dad's liver and that he likely had only a year left to live. There I sat with Dad's cousin and friend, neither of whom I knew well, hearing at age 21 that the Dad with whom I had just begun a special relationship, was now terminally ill.

I flew back to Brown, finished up exams, and went home for Christmas. Even home in Rochester with my family, there was no emotional support. Mom didn't want Sarah to know about Dad's cancer, thinking she was protecting her, and Mom herself was worried only about her future financial situation.

I did what I knew best, I internalized the feelings and turned to tennis as an outlet. I visited Dad a few weeks later. He was trying to regain his strength following his major surgery and subsequent complications requiring another hospitalization over the holidays. As soon as he could, he went back to work as General Counsel of the American Hospital Association while at the same time enduring chemotherapy treatments. Back at school, the only person who seemed to care about me was my tennis coach, because he would ask me how I was doing. I went on with my senior year, every other aspect of which was wonderful.

As graduation approached in May 1985, I told my parents I did not want to spend my graduation weekend having to divide my time between them. Dad's treatments were keeping him stable so the four of us convened in Providence to celebrate my graduation from Brown with a bachelor's degree in Psychology. We were able to spend the weekend together. My parents and Sarah would return to the hotel each evening and I would stay out late savoring my last days and nights of college.

I have told my children that the college years provide a bridge between childhood and adulthood. My Brown education was exactly what I needed to expand my horizons beyond the sheltered and controlled yet overall happy childhood in Rochester. I experienced monumental personal growth, made lifelong friends, sat by both my parents' sides during cancer surgery, and learned about myself, life, and my place in that life. I was sad to leave Brown but was excited and ready for the next chapter.

CHAPTER VI

———

On My Own

The law firm where I had worked the summer of 1984 offered me a full time position as Recruitment Coordinator following my college graduation. I was excited about moving to Washington, DC to live and work in the city where I had a positive experience the previous summer.

I went home to Rochester for the month of June to spend time with Mom and Sarah and prepare for my next adventure. Unfortunately, I had to have my wisdom teeth extracted during that time, but the physical pain from that procedure paled in comparison to the emotional pain I would experience at this time.

Mom bought a set of dishes for my new apartment, yet as I was preparing to embark at age 21 on my DC adventure, she told me to clear everything but the furniture out of my room, including the contents of my desk drawers. She said that if she couldn't have me at home, she didn't want reminders of me. That felt like a knife to my heart. The concept of home as a place for unconditional love was shattered. The hurt ran deep, yet I internalized those difficult emotions. Several years later, Mom said she was so depressed that I wasn't moving to Rochester permanently that she had been suicidal. Mom could have been proud of me going off with my Brown degree to start a great job in Washington. Instead, she treated me as if I were divorcing her, just as Dad had done 14 years earlier.

So off I went to make a life for myself in DC, fortunately equipped with all I had learned from the previous summer and with the understanding and support of my terminally ill father.

My first apartment was very simple, but I made it my home. My college trunk was my coffee table and wooden crates were my bookshelves. Dad shipped me some furniture he had in storage including a bed and a dresser, and a friend gave me an old couch which otherwise would have been discarded. My new home was in walking distance to the Metro which I took to and from work each day. I also was now in possession of Dad's old '78 black Oldsmobile Cutlass which I was able to park right outside my apartment. Dad helped me settle in as soon as I arrived and set up his old answering machine for me. He said in 1985 it was essential that, as a young single working woman, I should not miss any phone calls.

Dad continued to do well with his chemotherapy treatments and spent considerable time in DC working. We had dinner whenever he came to town and I would happily drive him to and from the airport. He was often working on cases with lawyers at the law firm where I worked. Dad was highly respected there and I was proud to be Richard Epstein's daughter.

I had friends in DC who had also moved there to work after college, though I often thought of the close friendships I had at Brown. I missed both my friends and college life. Often the people I worked with would invite me to join them for drinks and dinner. I was just out of college and they were mostly 30-something "yuppies"—young urban professionals, as they were called. I was happy to be included though they seemed much older. Many were recently married and buying their first home. There were also a few people closer to my age, single and living in apartments. Part of my job as Recruitment Coordinator was planning law firm social events. It was fun socializing with the people I worked with at events outside the office. Often senior partners would host everyone at their large, beautiful home or I would arrange firm outings such as a cocktail cruise along the Potomac River or an outdoor picnic with live music at an appropriate venue. I also played on the law firm softball team which always included going out with my work friends for drinks or a bite to eat after the game.

I played tennis occasionally with a friend from Western New York who had also moved to DC after college, a lawyer from the law firm who had played Division One college tennis, and new people I met. I was learning to live without my tennis identity and had to learn that I would be unable to maintain the level I had achieved in college.

I enjoyed attending DC professional sporting events and rooted for my new local teams. A highlight in the summer was sitting in box seats, courtesy of the law firm, at the professional tennis tournament that came to DC every summer. It was held at the same location where I had won a big local tournament the previous summer.

In August of 1985, Sarah came to visit when Dad was also in town. I saw over her shoulder as she wrote in her journal.

Betsy is a real grown up now.

The treatments were working. Dad felt good, but Sarah still had no idea how sick he was.

I loved the time Dad and I spent together in my new city, not just dinners out and social gatherings, but also time spent just the two of us, enjoying hanging out together in my apartment, going to a museum or a show, and building on the relationship that had begun only a year earlier. We enjoyed simple pleasures like cooking and eating together and trips to the hardware store.

Despite the intensity of the pain inflicted by Mom when I left Rochester, those feelings were suppressed within me with all the other difficult emotions, and I thought I would like to spend my 22nd birthday in Rochester with Mom and Sarah over Labor Day weekend. This idea did not sit well with Dad who was both angry with how Mom had treated me and proud of how well I was settling into my post-college life as an independent adult.

This morning I had a very upsetting conversation with Dad. I am sick of being in the middle between Mom and Dad. Dad is mad because I am going home this weekend. I'm going to go through this for every holiday. I love them both, I need them both, but I can't take this guilt they both lay on me. I see both their sides, but I can't please both of them. It makes me feel so alone.

The next day at work, Dad and I had another upsetting conversation.

Awful thoughts went through my head—suicide, getting in my car and just driving away .... Instead of doing something stupid, I went for a good, long run.

I wrote Dad a letter because I had an easier time expressing myself in writing.

All my life I've done things to try to please both of you and I've been there for both of you when you needed me. You both make your needs known to me, Mom in a subtle way and you more blatantly, but I feel like I can't say what I really want to say to either of you.

I ended up flying to Rochester to spend my 22nd birthday with Mom and Sarah. I wanted to do this, and I felt good being there despite knowing Dad disapproved.

I know there are issues I should bring up with Mom this weekend, but I'm scared to confront her, and I want to have a happy, special week-end. I love both my parents so much. It's not my fault they hate each other. Why do I have to be in the middle?

My birthday weekend in Rochester was wonderful and over the next several weeks I had several positive conversations with both Mom and Dad. I had a great job and an independent life in Washington, DC. I had people to play tennis with.

I played great, almost like my old self. It was such a good feeling. I do need tennis. I have friends to spend time with here but there is no one who knows Betsy Epstein and really cares.

My yuppie friends at the firm loved setting me up on dates with people they knew. These men were usually very nice and good for a date or two. Dad was right about the answering machine.

As a young single woman of the 1980s, it's great having an answering machine.

I loved grocery shopping *"especially when not in a hurry"* but journal entries often reflected a focus on body image.

I felt pretty and thin in my black cords.
I bought some jeans; they make me feel thin.

Yet, no eating disorder.

I enjoyed a fun weekend in New Jersey with my Brown tennis friends while they were competing at Princeton and I loved my first Brown homecoming weekend in Providence.

I miss Brown life so much

Overall, I had adjusted well to post-college life in Washington, DC but bouts of mild anxiety and depression were triggered by the issues with my parents and trying to figure out what I wanted to do with my life. I had always thought of myself as possibly going into clinical psychology or social work because I wanted to help children whose parents were divorced. Dad was starting to strongly urge me to consider law school instead.

Lately I have been confused about my future. Law school? Psych grad school? I wish I could decide if I want to go back to school.

Dad continued to look and feel well as he neared the one-year mark from his diagnosis.

Dad's CT Scan showed good news. The tumor is smaller and no further spread. What a relief. How can I get depressed when Dad has real things to worry about?

[handwritten: College, home, marriage, divorce, apartment, marriage, home; divorce]

Sometimes I felt I needed a good cry and other times I felt very happy. I was on an emotional rollercoaster ride.

> Sometimes I wonder what all this 1980s independence stuff is all about. Well, just like college was an adjustment, so is this. Right now, I'm on an emotional roller coaster. Hopefully soon I will adjust and be happy. I'm not unhappy now, just my usual confusion and mixed feelings.
>
> I started crying for no real reason. What is my problem?

And then:

> This week I have been feeling very happy. It's about time.

I'm sure these emotions were normal for someone at a transitional time in life as I was but as someone who always felt the need to be in control, this was not easy. I was an expert at internalizing rather than expressing my feelings and had only my journal to listen. *[handwritten: writing make me feel good]*

As the holidays approached, I expressed feelings of dread.

> I dread Thanksgiving and Christmas because of the decisions I will have to make. It's not fair for a child to have to decide between parents. There is no way I can please both of them, so, maybe I'll just spend them all alone.

As predicted, late Fall of 1985 brought one of my most difficult times, feeling caught in the middle between Mom and Dad. I had always spent Christmas with Mom and during my college years I also had celebrated Thanksgiving with her at home in Rochester. Mom was assuming that I would be home for both of these major holidays again, but now Dad was wanting me to spend Thanksgiving with him.

> Dad and I had a tearful talk about Thanksgiving. I feel a lot of pressure from Dad. I was so upset; I was almost sick to my stomach.

Mom had not yet seen my apartment or shown much interest in my Washington life, so I was thrilled when she said that she and Sarah would visit me for Thanksgiving.

Mom and Sarah are coming for Thanksgiving. I am so excited. I will clean in preparation and do the cooking and I will treat us to Thanksgiving dinner. I hope it will be a special week.

Dad was disappointed that I was not going to Chicago. I had felt so torn. I thought of driving away and not spending Thanksgiving with either of them. They could both worry about me. Dad had a new girlfriend, so I did not have to worry about him being alone for this holiday.

I excitedly prepared for Mom and Sarah's arrival by cleaning, cooking, planning activities, and researching the perfect place for Thanksgiving dinner reservations. The day before Thanksgiving Mom called to say they were going to New York instead because there was a chance Sarah could get into the doubles at a National tournament if she were there on site. She did not get into the singles. I was devastated. Without any consideration for my feelings, Mom wanted me to take the train to New York to join them.

Boy did I get upset. I had tearful talks with Mom and Dad. I know it's selfish, but I feel so hurt that Mom just cares about tennis and not at all about my feelings. I felt guilty for my selfish disappointment. Dad helped me feel better, but he thought I shouldn't go to New York. I knew I had to go to New York.

I took an early train to New York on Thanksgiving morning. Mom and I had a chance to talk at the hotel. She had answers for everything. I expressed to her that I had been thinking of spending Thanksgiving in Chicago with Dad because it could be his last. Mom responded with:

feeling guilty about my feelings if they hurt someone else.

Well, I could be hit by a truck.

Feeling deeply disappointed and hurt by the change in plans, I again suppressed the pain and upon returning to Washington, I wrote in my journal:

I feel guilty for my selfish disappointment. I realize what is important is that we were together, and I have a lot to be grateful for.

Mom must have felt badly for cancelling the Thanksgiving trip to Washington at the last minute because she and Sarah came to spend Christmas week with me. This was our first Christmas not in Rochester. I was excited for Mom to finally see my apartment where I had been living for five months. I cooked for Mom for the first time and planned many fun activities for our time together—tree decorating, museums, monuments, cozy nights hanging out together.

It was a very special week. I hope Mom enjoyed the week of vacation she so much deserved. We all enjoyed our time together.

At the end of our week together, Mom flew back to Rochester and Sarah and I flew to Florida to join Dad and his girlfriend to ring in the new year.

She is very nice but of course I feel like Dad ignored us.

Dad was experiencing unpleasant flashbacks from his cancer surgery the year before, but he passed the one-year mark feeling great, working hard, and living life to the fullest as 1985 came to an end. Looking at him, one would never know he was terminally ill.

The New Year 1986 started brilliantly for Dad. He spent significant time at the law firm where I worked preparing for his upcoming argument before the United States Supreme Court on behalf of the American Hospital Association. Dad and the other lawyers put in long hours. I would make sure he had his favorite Oreo cookies on hand. On January 15, 1986, I could not have been more proud watching my Dad arguing his case before the United States Supreme Court Justices. This was my first time in this impressive building, and I was in awe of Dad's astute legal skills. All the preparation at the firm was evident in his smooth presentation of the case and his articulate answering of the Justices interrogative questions. Dad's girlfriend was there with me. We all enjoyed a celebratory lunch after the argument.

Two days later, I learned that Dad and his girlfriend, Diana, were engaged.

This would be marriage number four. She helped to make the end of his life as happy as it could be. Dad worked for as long as he could, and they traveled extensively. Dad's impending marriage, however, left me with very mixed feelings even though she seemed wonderful and Dad was happy.

> *Dad and I have had such a special relationship these past two years and I'm scared of it changing. I'm worried he won't need me now that he has Diana. Dad reassured me that he still needs me.*

That winter we had many conversations about my future. I was still feeling conflicted about going to law school, as Dad wanted, or pursuing a graduate degree in Psychology, which had always interested me.

> *Dad helped me feel so much better about my career confusion. I don't know what I would do without him.*

During this time, one of the associates at the firm and I were becoming very good friends. We often went running together during lunch hour. He took an interest in me and seemed to really understand me.

> *Steve is so nice. He is like a big brother, friend, confidante.*

I had no idea at this time how important my relationship with Steve and his wife Patti would become in my life.

I continued to have a challenging relationship with Mom but would meet her and Sarah for weekends at Sarah's tournaments in New York.

> *Although Mom and I don't have the same relationship we used to, it was still a wonderful weekend. I love being with them and miss them when I'm not.*

Yet, I would have very upsetting phone conversations with Mom.

> *Mom feels I don't want her a part of my life and she's mad about my relationship with Dad.*

At this stage, I felt that Dad really understood me. We spent time together in DC, so he had firsthand knowledge of my daily life. He knew I was struggling with my decision about going back to school and he patiently listened to me and talked through the options.

> *I so much enjoyed time with Dad today, not doing anything special but just spending time together.*

After many conversations with Dad and much indecision on my part, I came to the realization that law school made a lot of sense.

> *There seems to be no reason against going to law school. Dad made me feel very reassured. Take it one step at a time.*

Two months before Dad's small wedding, which was scheduled to take place in my apartment, Dad received the devastating news that his chemotherapy treatments were no longer working. He looked and felt well, but the chemotherapy that had enabled him to live far beyond the original one-year prognosis was no longer able to keep his terminal cancer stable.

> *I get sad thinking about life without Dad, completely on my own in the real world.*
> *What will I do without my source of strength and support? I'm supposedly a mature adult but in a lot of ways I'm still a little girl who needs a daddy.*

I began the six weeks of preparatory classes for the Law School Admission Test (LSAT). The class met for several hours in the evening after a full day of work. On top of this, I needed to do as many practice questions as possible on my own.

> *Part of me felt like what are you doing here and the other part of me said if you work hard you can do well.*

Just before Dad's early June wedding, he learned he had been accepted into an experimental treatment program at the National Institutes of Health, located in Maryland, just outside Washington, DC. We would have even more time together. The firm where I worked allowed me to take whatever time I needed to help Dad. I drove him to and from all his appointments and did whatever he needed me to do for him.

It means so much to me that Dad cares so much about me

In June 1986, the wedding took place just before the clinical trials began. Dad married for the fourth time on a beautiful early June weekend. Sarah flew in for the weekend and for a couple of days we could forget about Dad's cancer. Looking back, Diana made the end of his life as happy as it could be. They made the most of every day.

I wore my new pink dress. I felt pretty and thin.

[handwritten: Focus on food instead of her sadness about her dad.]

After a big celebratory dinner, the evening before the wedding I wrote in my journal:

I shouldn't have eaten so much.

The wedding itself went as planned. Dad and Diana seemed so happy. Yet,

I felt no particular emotions.

Within days after the wedding, we learned that Dad, on behalf of the American Hospital Association, had won the case he had argued five months earlier before the United States Supreme Court. There were several celebratory dinners with the attorneys involved in the case, and I was always included.

I took the LSAT and received a very respectable score. The first step towards law school was complete. The next step would be to request and complete law school applications.

Dad and I had a chance to talk alone. I sense Dad really wants me to go to law school.

How does one go against the wishes of one's dying father? Dad began the clinical trials that summer of 1986. During treatment weeks I was with him as much as possible. Diana worked in Chicago and came out when she could. Aside from treatment weeks, Dad was also working in Chicago.

> *I'm worried because Dad doesn't look that well. I hope this experimental treatment is all worth it. I am scared for him.*

At times that summer I could be a normal 22-year-old. One of my best friends from college spent the summer of 1986 interning in Washington, DC. We went out almost every day after work often late into the evening. This was the perfect escape from confronting the reality of Dad's declining health and the anxiety about law school.

In late June, I went back to Rochester for a weekend to happily attend my fifth high school reunion.

> *I was proud answering questions about my life.*

As the summer went on, and as Dad endured the clinical trials, he was becoming more and more depressed.

> *Dad is not in good spirits. I know he is scared. I feel helpless. I wish I could do something.*

Physically, he was often fatigued and at times had a slight fever. I drove Dad to and from the NIH Clinic during treatment weeks.

> *I don't know what to say to dad. I want more than anything to cheer him up. I know he is scared.*

We would eat dinner in the evening following his long, difficult days at the clinic. I would prepare whatever he felt like eating. Sometimes it was simply a bowl of soup or when he was feeling well enough, we would go out.

> *I wish I could eat without feeling guilty.*

eating because of unhappiness
food will take my mind off worries

This was clearly an emotional time and except for an occasional cry, I stayed strong which I thought meant staying positive and unemotional.

When summer was nearing its end and my friend who had made for some very happy summer memories left DC, I headed back to Rochester to celebrate my 23rd birthday with Mom and Sarah. Nothing had changed at home, yet I was still drawn to time there, especially for my birthday which Mom had always made special. At times, Mom was very loving and other times there was the same tension I had felt many times before. My journal comments ranged from "*I hate Mom's money problems*" to "*My birthday dinner was fun, and I felt special.*"

I still wanted and needed for Rochester to be home, a place for unconditional love. While I did feel loved, I also felt that whenever I returned, I somehow had to fit back into Mom's bubble. Appeasing Mom and internalizing my feelings was easier than risking upsetting her and increasing her moodiness.

I returned to DC after my 23rd birthday trip that early September of 1986 to the difficult reality that Dad's cancer was taking over and the experimental treatment was not helping. The program had given Dad hope, but now all the signs indicated that any hope we had was dashed.

Dad called—he has an ongoing fever and doesn't feel well. I feel so badly for him. He might not continue in the program.

During this stressful time, I was grateful for the support of my good friend, Steve, at the law firm. I felt he understood me, and we had great talks about Dad and law school when we went running together.

Though Dad's health was deteriorating rapidly, we were able to have important conversations and he was able to read and comment on the draft of my personal essay that I had written as part of my law school applications.

Dad and I talked for a few hours. We talked a lot about law school. When I listen to him there is no doubt that I should go to law school. I still have a hard time convincing myself.

We also had conversations about the estate planning he had done earlier on in his illness. Talking about what would happen after he was gone was difficult, yet that time was fast approaching.

Dad returned to DC one last time later in September and, though he was not well, he ate a lasagna dinner I made for him in my apartment.

I picked up Daddy at the airport. I don't think he's doing very well. He just started crying at one point saying he's depressed.

He officially left the NIH program and went home to Chicago. I tried to focus on work, but the frequent updates about Dad were very upsetting.

Diana called to tell me Daddy was feeling worse today and in pain. I feel so helpless. Cancer takes control and there's nothing anyone can do.

During this difficult time, Steve and his wife Patti were caring and supportive. They always took time to ask how I was doing and would listen to the answer.

I broke down in Steve's office. I don't know what I would do without him. So much is building up inside me and I feel guilty being upset.

I started spending the night with Steve and Patti up on the third floor of their house. I was becoming as close to Patti as I was to Steve. They helped me feel safe and secure.

She gave me a big hug, my first one since all this and boy did I need it. They are the best friends I could ever have. I feel I don't deserve it.

Diana called to tell me that Dad was now experiencing confusion, memory loss, and was having trouble finding his words. His cousin said he had not more than a few more weeks to live.

I felt no emotions, just numb. There are so many unresolved issues I need to handle, namely Mom's financial situation and Sarah's knowing. Mom has no idea what Dad means to me.

There was much on my mind and so much responsibility on my shoulders at just 23 years old.

I must be awful to be around. I wish I could have a good cry to feel better.

The next weekend, I flew out to Chicago to see Dad. Mom finally told Sarah, now 16, how sick Dad was, and she let Sarah fly to Chicago for just over 24 hours to say her goodbyes.

Dad had left us when Sarah was a baby and she only knew life in Mom's bubble. Dad had taken Sarah on many wonderful trips and he had taught her to drive six months earlier on a visit to Rochester. She would miss out on having an independent relationship with him as I had been blessed to have the past two years. Now Sarah had to say goodbye to her Dad without time to process the fact that he was terminally ill. Mom thought she had been protecting her by withholding the truth, but she made it harder and more overwhelming.

Sarah and I sat on the couch both apprehensive about seeing Dad. Sarah started crying and we hugged each other.

The next day, Sarah had to say her goodbyes to the Dad she was just starting to get to know. I promised Sarah that I would try to do everything for her that Dad would have done.

Sarah spent some time with Dad saying goodbye. She cried and I comforted her.

Then she went back to Mom's bubble.

I did not leave Dad after the weekend. The senior partners of the law firm had deep respect for him and one of them was a dear friend. I was encouraged to stay in Chicago as long as I needed to and not to worry about anything at work.

It hurts seeing Dad like this but it's comforting not being so far away. Tonight, I started crying and it was hard to stop. There was no one to comfort me.

Diana said she was glad I was there, but she had to go to work every day. I was there with Dad in the condo along with a private duty hospice nurse who was there to care for him.

It hurt so much to see him so uncomfortable when the morphine was wearing off.

Steve called daily to check on me. I was becoming emotionally dependent on him. He reassured me I was doing the right thing by staying in Chicago. I needed to hear that because Mom had made me feel guilty about missing work.

I wish Mom understood.

I spent a lot of time sitting by Dad's bed feeding him soup and just holding his hand. I know that he knew I was there.

Dad told me he loves me, and he doesn't like to argue with me.

He was very thin, confused, and with few exceptions unable to express himself. He asked Diana why I was there, and he kept asking what happened. His pain was controlled by more and more morphine, but he had occasional lucid moments amid the confusion. As cancer took over his body, he eventually slept more and more.

Dad and Diana lived in a beautiful high-rise condo building on Chicago's famed Lake Shore Drive. While Dad slept, I would stare at beautiful and vast Lake Michigan several stories below and as far as the eyes could see. I went on long runs along the lake front path listening to my favorite "Simply Red" cassette tape in my Walkman. This was a good outlet for difficult emotions. In the evening Diana and I ate dinner together, the meal often dropped off by her friends. We would watch TV together. She was very kind to me. The phone rang constantly with concerned friends asking how Dad was doing. We patiently responded to the same questions over and over with the same sad answers.

I found moments of peace by the lake both inside the condo and outside on my runs, but I neither knew how to articulate or express how I was feeling.

I am so messed up in my head. Sometimes I feel fine, sometimes uptight, sometimes upset.

After many days of sitting by Dad's bedside, evenings with Diana, daily phone conversations with Steve, and frequent phone calls from concerned friends and colleagues of Dad, I felt it was time to return to Washington, DC. Dad was kept comfortable with increasing doses of morphine. The awake time was less and less each day as he slept more and more. The hospice nurse provided wonderful care. Before my flight back to DC on a beautiful Saturday evening, I spent the last possible minutes with my dying father.

I spent a lot of time with Dad. I told him I was leaving and that I loved him. I can't believe this was the last time I would see my father alive. I cried when I was sitting with him. He kissed me and hugged me, and I held his hand.

Steve and Patti were there for me when I returned to Washington, and I continued to stay with them. Steve reassured me I would never be alone.

I have become so dependent on them. I hope I can get back to being a mature independent adult.

On some level, being back at work and in some kind of routine was helpful. Everyone at the law firm was kind and caring but the only real support came in the evenings with Steve and Patti who so graciously made me feel comfortable staying in their home. I received no support at all from Mom who, whenever I called, seemed more interested in tennis than me. She only cared about her future financial situation after Dad's death.

In Chicago, not much had changed as Dad neared the end of his life.

The nurse put Dad on the phone, He sounded so weak but asked me where I was and if I was okay.

October 28, 1986, nearly two months after my 23rd birthday, colon cancer took the life of my 56-year-old father. As I write this sentence, I am 56 years old.

A day I will never forget. He's gone . . . Dad died at 6:30 p.m. Chicago time. I didn't cry and still haven't.

I learned the inevitable news in Steve's office at the end of a late work-day. I called Mom and Sarah and went "home" with Steve. He and Patti stayed up with me until midnight.

The two years I had with Dad at his end of life were a gift for which I would always be grateful. Dad mellowed as he knew his time was limited. He no longer lectured or criticized me but instead taught me so much about life and appreciated me for the independent young adult I had become. His last gift was impressing upon me the value and marketability of a law degree. I flew back to Chicago as arrangements were underway to celebrate and honor the life and legacy of Richard Lewis Epstein.

The apartment feels empty without Dad here. I can't even just watch him sleep or look at him or hug him or hold his hand like before.

Sarah flew to Chicago too, but on the phone, Mom spoke as if she were only coming because she was supposed to be there and not because she felt anything.

Her attitude really bothers me.

The funeral took place on Halloween, three days after Dad died. There were at least 200 people there. Friends and colleagues flew in from around the country and expressed their sorrow to Diana, Sarah, and me in a private room before the service began. I sobbed through most of the service never turning around to see all the people who were there because Dad had an impact on their lives in some way. Sarah read a beautiful poem that she had written. I was grateful that Steve and a close friend from college were there to support me. Afterwards, with all the people back at the condo talking and eating, it seemed more like a party. Dad, who was always the life of the party, would have loved seeing all the important people in his personal and professional life there together.

In the evening, Steve, my college friend, Sarah, and I went for a walk on the clear, warm October night. That time together was meaningful after being with many of Dad's friends and colleagues whom I did not know. I had to say goodbye to my circle of support as they flew their separate ways the next morning. Dad decided before he died that he would be cremated with his ashes buried in his family plot in Northern New Jersey.

I stayed for a few extra days after the funeral. Diana and I went through some of Dad's things and I had to decide what I would bring back to DC with me.

> We cried a lot and talked openly. I am bringing so much stuff with me. I feel like I am taking it from him—like I don't believe he's gone forever.

I took breaks to run along the beautiful lake shore. The nights of sleeping very little were catching up with me and I started to feel lethargic, exhausted, and was coming down with a cold. I did not know then that grief affects one on every level, including physically.

For my last night in Chicago some close friends of Dad, with whom I had happy memories from visits many years prior, came over with lots of food. Their presence was comforting, yet, at one point, I felt myself starting to cry. I ran into the other room.

> I guess this is grieving. I had no one to comfort me. I hugged the stuffed bear my stepmother had given me several weeks earlier. I got control of myself and rejoined everyone. *don't know how to grieve and feel so I internalize things, get angry,*

I couldn't begin to understand at that time that crying and feeling out of control were a necessary and normal part of grieving. All I knew was how to suppress and internalize difficult emotions. Later in the evening, Sarah called.

> I said hello to Mom, but she was **very** cold toward me.

The next day, I dressed cozily in one of Dad's sweaters for my flight home to DC. I felt sad saying goodbye to Diana.

> She seemed really sad. I wish I could help her. I hope she will be okay.

Steve picked me up at the airport upon my return home. I was exhausted and generally feeling lousy. I packed a bag at my apartment and went back to stay in the comfort of Steve and Patti's home, surrounded by their love and support.

I realize how lucky I am to have them as such special friends.

At age 23, with my Dad having just died, my surviving parent offered no support. This was hurtful.

I called Mom and was very angry when we hung up. For one thing, she told me she is giving up long distance phone calls because of the money and she didn't seem to understand why I wasn't back at work or staying at my own apartment.

I did some errands but was feeling very "mopey."

I hate feeling like that. I was fine before I talked to Mom. I feel so guilty saying bad things about her.

In about a week, I was back at my own apartment and felt ready to return to work.

I was happy to be going back and felt so professional carrying Dad's small leather briefcase. Everyone was so nice. It felt good to be back and I was busy all day.

My close friendship with Steve and Patti continued to sustain me, and I continued to sleep over occasionally at their home on the weekend. Dad had read my law school essay before he died and now it was time to work on my applications. I was continuing the process one step at a time as Dad had wisely advised, but I remained uncertain and unable to picture myself in law school.

I have been eating a lot lately. I don't want to gain weight, but I don't want to be preoccupied with calories either.

again, preoccupation with food, keeps her from confronting anxiety about law school.

No eating disorder symptoms, but journal entries like this one show a focus on food, especially during times when I was trying to cope with difficult emotions.

I think of Dad so much. I really miss him—part of my life is missing.

I was making progress with my law school applications and mailed several by Thanksgiving—another step in the process. I went to Rochester for Thanksgiving. Though I was looking forward to seeing Mom and Sarah, and happy to be having Thanksgiving dinner at the home of our close friends, there was little to no talk about Dad whose death was less than a month earlier. The only reference to his death was in the context of Mom's financial woes.

> *I'm glad I went home for Thanksgiving. On the surface, everything was great. There is unspoken subtle tension between Mom and me. I felt I could not express any emotion and I didn't receive any tender loving care which is what I need, more than anything—to be taken care of emotionally. I feel guilty thinking these things because they are my family—the only one I have, and I love them deeply.*

In the weeks that followed, I had my work routine to keep me busy and I felt very comfortable with everyone at the firm. I finished my law school applications and tried to have a social life once again. I felt happiest when with Steve and Patti, because I could be honest about my feelings. Steve always said, "Your feelings are your feelings." Many years would pass before I could express negative feelings without guilt. I thought of Dad constantly and missed our time together. I missed not only his company but his guidance and advice.

> *I miss him so much. I need him.*
> *The pain is almost unbearable at times.*

Mom and Sarah came to Washington, DC for Christmas, as they had done the previous year. On so many levels we had a wonderful time celebrating

Christmas and enjoying DC tourist activities together, but there was the unspoken tension that remained between Mom and me.

> *She still has no idea how Dad's death has affected me. I need a mom to be a parent, give me TLC, understand what I am feeling. Mom and Sarah don't care that Dad is gone.*

Sometimes I would write "letters" to Dad after his death to express to him how much I missed him. In December 1986, just two months after his death, I wrote:

> *Two months have gone by since you died. I feel like I'm supposed to be okay. Everyone assumes I am, but I'm not. I'm scared something is wrong with me. I feel like I am not being a good person.*

Reading letters like that, over 30 years later, makes me wish I could give 23-year-old Betsy a big hug and get her an appointment with a licensed mental health professional.

The start of 1987 brought more sadness as loss and the reality of Dad's death became the focus of my thoughts. I continued to enjoy my work at the law firm and Steve and Patti continued to be my source of comfort and support and friendship. I stayed with them less frequently but when a huge snowstorm blanketed the area, I was thrilled to be snowed in with them. Steve always asked me how I was feeling, and I could answer truthfully. Patti gave the best hugs and always seemed to know when I needed one.

> *I have been feeling depressed, alone, not looking forward to anything, scared something is wrong with me. I even mentioned how the thought crossed my mind that if I were dead, I would be able to be with Dad.*

These thoughts were scary, indicating depression. My journal reveals my deepest thoughts and the depth of my despair in January of 1987.

> *I have everything to be grateful for. I am down on myself for feeling down and unmotivated. Dad was an inspiration, just talking to him*

made me feel motivated. His visits always gave me something to look forward to. He always loved me through good and bad, I didn't have to be perfect. I miss him so much. I feel lost without him and devoid of my happy, secure self. I know eventually I'll be stronger from all this but right now it is consuming me.

On the one-year anniversary of Dad's Supreme Court argument, I drove by the Supreme Court thinking about what a special day that was and how proud I was to be his daughter.

I asked God to tell Dad I love him and that I hope he is resting peacefully. My, what can happen in a year.

In early February of 1987, I received my first law school acceptance!

I burst out crying—I wanted more than anything to call Dad. I called Mom and she seemed pleased.

The step by step process towards law school marched on. My first acceptance made me pleased yet I had never officially decided on going to law school.

I'm scared—I wish I could talk to Dad, especially about my law school decision. I don't feel sad or depressed—just full of thought—so much going on in my head.

As winter turned to spring, I was doing better emotionally. I loved my job, played tennis occasionally, went on a few dates and enjoyed time with friends. I was able to travel to a work conference and visit close college friends.

I needed this weekend so much—emotionally being with my close friends and a break from my yuppie, Washington real world I live in.

I seemed to be shopping more and still felt guilty when spending money on myself. I worried that I was becoming materialistic and trying to "buy my happiness." When I described a new outfit I was wearing, I often followed it with "*I felt pretty.*" There were fewer comments that included "*and thin.*"

In addition to traveling, I also welcomed visits from good friends and loved sharing my city with them. Mom and Sarah visited in late March during Sarah's spring break and we took some of that time to visit colleges in the Southeast since Sarah was now a junior in high school and interested in colleges up and down the East Coast. We laughed a lot and enjoyed our time together. However, when Mom was at home, she seemed distant and not interested in me. I would hope for phone calls from her.

> *Mom doesn't call me because I have more money than she has. She thinks her role as a parent ended when I turned 21. Oh well. I have to be strong because this is how things were meant to be.*

The issues with Mom further reinforced how alone I felt without Dad who had started behaving like a parent to me two years before his death.

> *Dad was unique and played a special role in my life. I feel alone. I need love and care and understanding.*

Though I still could not picture myself at law school, I put down a deposit to hold a spot at American University in Washington, DC. While at first it had seemed appealing to experience a new area for three years of law school, now after all I had been through with dad's death, I was not ready to uproot myself and start over. I especially could not imagine leaving Steve and Patti, my only support system.

Though life was busy and generally happier, my journal reveals that I often cried myself to sleep in the months following Dad's death. Appearing to be "strong" and keeping it together during the day took a toll when alone at night, and the tears flooded my pillow.

> *I cried myself to sleep. There is so much built up inside me. I want dad to be proud of how I am.*

On April 26, 1987, Dad would have turned 57 years old.

It's Dad's birthday. I asked God to wish him a happy birthday for me.
I miss him. I need to talk to him.

I made sure I ate one of Dad's favorite meals, tuna fish on a bagel.

In early May, I joined Diana and Dad's cousins for the burial of Dad's ashes at the family cemetery plot in New Jersey.

I cried so hard. I had never seen the urn containing my Dad's ashes.
It's hard to believe a man so alive as my Dad was now ashes.

I spent more time with Diana before taking the train back to DC.

I felt so drained and emotionally and physically exhausted.

The next day I talked to Mom and told her I was upset.

I couldn't really explain it and she wouldn't understand it anyway.

The idea of law school was becoming more real. I had officially registered to attend starting in August, but mixed feelings remained after visiting the campus.

In some ways I want the challenge and I know I would be wimping
out by staying where I feel secure and not trying to achieve something.
I'm so confused. I need to talk to Dad.

Though I continued to cry myself to sleep many nights, summer had arrived, and I was feeling happier. I was definitely going to law school, and my last day at the law firm would be July 24th. I loved warm summer nights in Washington and I finally felt more like a 23-year-old again, going out several nights a week after work, enjoying friends, late nights, and even a summer fling.

I was so happy and content and appreciative of each moment. It's so
nice being with a good friend. I wish I could relay this kind of day to
Dad.

I traveled to Brown for graduation weekend and thoroughly enjoyed my good friends, late night parties, and a mini-tennis team reunion lunch.

> *What a wonderful weekend. In a way I'm mad at myself for abusing my body with so little sleep and alcohol, but it felt good to be a little carefree and have fun. Brown really is a special place. I only wish I had taken advantage of it sooner.*

I also spent a long weekend in June in Rochester with Mom and Sarah.

> *It means so much that Mom has been acting more interested in my life. I should have been so happy. Why do I cry so easily?*

Though I no longer stayed over at Steve and Patti's, I treasured the time we spent together. Steve and I often went running together at lunch time and on weekends I would sometimes be invited to join them for dinner and a movie. Patti continued to sense when I needed a hug and they both always gave me good advice, listened to me, and understood me better than anyone.

> *Together with all my happiness, I still feel some sadness. There is so much I want to share with Dad, and I feel so badly that he can't enjoy summer—his favorite time of year. I think of everything he went through. I wish I could thank him for all he did for me.*

July 1987 brought the end of my tenure as law firm recruitment coordinator. I was showered with well wishes, lunches, flowers, cake, and gifts. Saying goodbye to so many wonderful work friends was made easier because I was staying in DC for law school. During my two years there, I learned about daily operations in a law firm, gained confidence in myself, and felt fortunate to go to work each day. As my first non-tennis related job, it made possible my life as an independent adult in Washington, DC. I loved being Richard Epstein's daughter there, but more importantly I had proved myself as smart, capable, and successful beyond the classroom and tennis court. I would miss the daily routine, but I was looking forward to time off before the start of law school.

Besides traveling to Lake George, New York, and Hilton Head, South Carolina, my break entailed moving into a new apartment in a great neighborhood, close to the law school and also not too far from Steve and Patti's house. I was excited too, because a close friend from Brown was moving to DC and would be my roommate. Steve and Patti helped with all the details for leasing my new apartment and Diana came from Chicago to help with the move and getting settled in my new home, along with Steve and Patti. Though I felt so materialistic, I used money Dad had left me to purchase needed things for my apartment such as a bed, couch, and VCR. I also bought a new car, a 1987 silver Volkswagen Jetta. Dad's old '78 Oldsmobile was starting to need more and more expensive repairs.

Always feels she doesn't deserve things

I feel so fortunate to be moving into such a wonderful apartment. I feel like I don't deserve it.

Following my travels, I enjoyed time to myself setting up my new apartment and catching up in my journal after being with friends. I happily welcomed my college friend to our apartment and DC. Mom even sent a note saying she was proud of me for starting law school and also said to pick out a desk which would be her gift to me. Her note meant much to me. After a difficult past year, it had been a great summer.

I was thinking about what a fun and innocent summer I had, but then I felt scared thinking about what will happen next. I have such a need for stability.

On the night before law school, I wanted more than anything to talk to Dad.

I hope I am ready for tomorrow—the first day of a new stage in my life.

Constant ache and missing her dad

———

CHAPTER VII

Law School: The First Year

In August of 1987, just weeks before my 24th birthday, I started my first year at American University's Washington College of Law. The campus was located in a suburban area of Washington, DC, a short drive from my new apartment.

Upon awakening on the morning of registration and orientation, my thoughts immediately turned to Dad whose death was less than a year prior to this important day. The stuffed bear to which I had become attached for comfort around the time of Dad's death gave me a sign.

> *A funny thing happened when I opened my eyes. My bear was on its side with a cute smile looking at me. It was a symbol to me that Dad was with me and knew what today was.*

I was nervous and excited as I left my apartment for the ten-minute drive to school on that first morning.

> *I wish I could have heard Dad's pep talk. I hope I can handle law school.*

In line at registration, I quickly became friends with a woman from a town near Rochester. We were happy to learn that we would be in the same classes this first year. We spent orientation together learning not only about the first-year of law school, but also about each other.

It feels so good to have a friend already.

Dad must have known what he was doing in strongly encouraging me to attend law school because, though I would not yet know this, I also met in line at registration the man I would eventually marry. His name was Jeff Brenner and he too would be in all my first year classes.

At orientation, the Dean of the Law School advised us to clear our heads intellectually and emotionally.

I can do the first but not the second.

I was pleased that Mom called to see how my first day went though she cut the conversation short because she was paying for the call.

I guess it's Dad I really want to talk to about law school. Am I doing this for me?

The required first year classes included: Torts, Contracts, Property, Civil Procedure, and a legal writing and skills class called Legal Methods. The first-year class was divided into three sections and we had all our classes with our same section of students. My professors ranged from a new young handsome professor to an older veteran professor who strongly believed in the Socratic method, calling on students randomly and drilling them with questions about the cases assigned for the day. I never felt comfortable speaking in class and I especially feared being called on in law school. The best classes were those where the professor told students in advance the day they would be called on, so there would be opportunity to be extra well-prepared for that day's cases.

My new friend and I established a nice routine, spending time between classes eating lunch together, doing our reading, browsing in the campus store, and just chatting. Also, Jeff and I were both the type who arrived early to the first class of the day so we would have friendly conversations.

The workload was heavy right from the start. In addition to reading numerous cases for each class and "briefing" them as we were instructed, we also had many assignments for our Legal Methods class which taught us how to write as lawyers, cite cases, and use the Law Library effectively.

Law school is tough. I have such a love-hate relationship with it. It does feel good to be learning again and have the feeling of accomplishment.

At the end of each day before going to sleep, I took time to express my thoughts and recount my day in my journal.

I shouldn't let myself get run down. I was up so late when I have to get up early. But I need to unwind after a long day and lying on my bed writing is very therapeutic.

Mom and Sarah came to visit me in late August for an early birthday celebration, and I was grateful we got along so well.

I felt so happy being with my family. I felt appreciative of the day and grateful to be alive. It was sad saying goodbye at the airport. What a great weekend. It felt good to feel loved and be hugged.

When my actual birthday came days later, I felt a letdown not being with Mom and Sarah.

Birthdays have always been so special in my family. I guess at 24 I can't expect to have that anymore. I felt so loved and so happy when they were here.

For the first time in my life, I had classes on my birthday. After my last class, I walked around my wonderful neighborhood which was filled with stores of all kinds and restaurants.

I felt so content with the world and guilty for how I felt before.

I ended up having a wonderful birthday evening at Steve and Patti's house. They spoiled me with an amazing dinner and wonderful gifts. My roommate was there too for the celebration.

It turned out to be an extra special birthday. I feel so guilty for the selfish thoughts I felt earlier.

Despite managing the heavy workload and adjusting to being a student again, there were opportunities for fun during those first weeks of law school. My roommate and I travelled to New Jersey for the wedding of one of our Brown tennis teammates.

It was a very special afternoon being with all my former teammates.

The best break, however, from my new reality was time spent with Steve and Patti. I now lived only a few streets from them so getting together was easy. Sometimes I joined them for dinner and a movie. Other times I hung out at their house or joined Steve for a weekend run or a long walk with their dog. A popular eatery in the neighborhood was Booey Monger where we would meet for coffee and carrot cake or frozen yogurt.

I feel secure when I am with Steve and Patti. My life is so different now from when I used to stay there. It's hard to explain how I feel. Patti gave me a big hug goodbye. I love them so much.

As lawyers themselves, Steve and Patti were a tremendous source of support as I navigated the stresses of those early weeks of law school. They certainly understood what I was facing and were there for me for advice and encouragement.

I know law school is supposed to be stressful. I better get used to it. I don't mean to feel sorry for myself. No one forced me to go to law school. Now I have to accept the responsibility.

Day to day, I had a nice routine. I had my good friend at school to be with between classes and I came home each day to one of my best friends from college. I ran almost every day, not only for exercise, but also as a healthy outlet for stress. I was a conscientious student but also made time for keeping in touch with friends and relaxing in front of my favorite television shows. I often got my best studying done when I would accompany Steve to his office when he had work to do on the weekends.

I wished for calls from Mom, perhaps longing for support I knew I would not get.

> *I wish Mom would call me. We haven't talked for a week. I would wait until she calls but if I want to talk to her, I can't do that.*

When I did talk to her, the conversation was often more frustrating than positive.

> *Mom and I were talking about law school and she seemed to be questioning my decision to go to law school. Whenever I mentioned how tough it was, she would remind me that it was my choice to go. She even went as far as to "joke" about my quitting law school and moving home.*

I knew she was not joking. The parent, who would have been proud of me and who would have given the support and encouragement I needed, was dead.

About two months into law school, I was feeling overwhelmed.

> *It's after midnight and I am trying to recover from a mini-breakdown. I don't feel well physically, and I feel overwhelmed with work. I started to cry, walking to my car.*

Though I was into the law school routine and recognized and accepted, the demands law school required intellectually, and time wise, at this time I was questioning myself and wondering if I had made a huge mistake.

I feel I am trying to please Dad, but he can't give me the support in return. If I quit, I would feel like such a failure. I am trying to please everyone, but I don't know what pleases me.

Fortunately, I made it through that stressful time and was able to stay on track. I recommitted myself and focused on completing the assignments which were making me feel so overwhelmed. I may have been motivated by the fear of failure instilled in me long ago. I also knew that I could accomplish anything I set my mind to do. In both high school and college, I managed challenging academics while balancing my tennis career. Now it was academics only demanding my attention. Before I knew it, I was halfway through my first semester and handling it well.

I keep thinking about things I can't express to anyone about last year. I'm trying to be strong and keep all those feelings to myself.

Mom remembered the one-year anniversary date of Dad's death and actually called me.

She sounded like she had been crying. For some reason, with her, I was very unemotional. Her call meant so much to me but part of me felt like "where have you been all year."

To mark the one-year anniversary, I lit a candle in Dad's memory.

The candle burns in memory of a very special person—my Dad, a unique individual whose charm, love, wit, intelligence, and courage I will never forget. The bad times, all the pain and hurt, are overshadowed by all the happy memories of the last few years. What a special relationship developed.

I continued to cry myself to sleep at times. In my limited free time, I worked on putting together a memory album with pictures, cards, and special mementos of times with Dad.

I cried hard which felt good. It helps ease the pain.

My life took a monumental turn shortly after the one-year anniversary of Dad's death. I started spending more time with Jeff Brenner. We both attended some Sports and Entertainment Law programs at the law school and we played tennis together a few times. After one of our times together, he asked if I wanted to have dinner. We went to Booey Monger, a neighborhood café. We had deep, serious conversations about my Dad's death, grief, and Jeff's college fraternity brother who had died by suicide the previous spring. I gave him a ride to his apartment after dinner.

When I dropped Jeff off, he said he really enjoyed talking with me and that he hadn't had any serious talks since he got here. I really like him. Who knows if anything will develop.

Our first official date was a few weeks later on November 6, 1987. Jeff had called to ask me out and I didn't want to decline for fear he wouldn't ask again. So, on our first date we were joined by my friend with whom I already had made plans for a movie night. The three of us went to the movie theatre to see the movie *Baby Boom*. When we were alone later that evening, Jeff said he thought I was cute when he saw me in line at registration on the very first day.

Given the demands of law school, much of our time together outside of class was spent studying together. Jeff was extremely studious and thus a very good influence on me. When he wasn't there in the evenings, I often would hang out and talk with my roommate.

Tonight, I didn't feel like studying. Where is my self-discipline?

Jeff and I spent lots of time together, had many real conversations, and became close very quickly. I thought about him when we were not together, and I always looked forward to seeing him.

One time Jeff thoughtfully brought over a sugary, frosted coffee cake for us to share. Instead of feeling happy about his nice gesture, the brewing eating disorder voice still deep inside me reacted negatively. I could never eat something like that and I didn't think Jeff should either. I kept my feelings to myself and only Jeff enjoyed the coffee cake.

I told my roommate all about Jeff and she gave me her approval which, as one of my closest friends, was important to hear. She said:

> He's really nice and has a certain charm to him. You seem so comfortable together.

Jeff and I were comfortable together, and when Steve asked if I was happy, I responded "Yes, I guess I am."

> I couldn't believe all this was happening but at the same time I felt content, comfortable, and relaxed.

Jeff and I were officially a couple, but I still valued my independence.

> Part of me is in such need of affection and caring but another part of me has gotten strong, tough, and able to be alone just fine.

I didn't understand that independence and inner strength could co-exist with a close and significant relationship. I was not giving up anything but rather adding so much to my life.

> I'm so glad we feel comfortable talking to each other about things. At a quiet moment Jeff asked me what I was thinking. I hesitated but said I was thinking about how happy I am and that I am feeling in love.

Jeff responded with "I love you, Betsy" and confided that he had never said that to anyone before. By this time, Jeff had said many times that he wished I would open up more. I had difficulty letting my guard down, and in hindsight I'm sure this was due to the hurt I had experienced.

Jeff helped me to feel comfortable and gradually I opened up more. He was also patient and understanding when I was feeling sad or emotional.

I was in one of my mellow moods. I don't know what caused it. Maybe it's being happy and not being able to share it with Dad. I really feel the pain.

I still treasured my time with Steve and Patti. I had a great conversation with Steve about how comfortable I felt with Jeff and how I am starting to let my guard down.

I feel so happy, secure, and content. I'll always need Steve. He understands me better than anyone.

I had a small dinner party for Jeff to meet Steve and Patti. The evening was a success.

What a relief to have Steve and Patti's approval.

When Thanksgiving break arrived toward the end of our first semester, Jeff traveled home to his family in Rhode Island and I went to Rochester. Sarah was away at a tournament, so Mom and I had a few days alone together. While we enjoyed shopping, good eating, and nightly Scrabble games, the visit was not without anger, stress, and difficult emotions. I even had to go out to a store and buy a toothbrush because Mom had thrown mine out. I didn't bring one with me because of course I still thought of Rochester as some semblance of home.

When Sarah called from her tournament in Kansas, I happened to answer the phone and we chatted happily. Mom stood right next to me demanding that I give her the phone. She kept saying "I'm paying for the call. She's my baby."

I was so angry. Mom totally lives through Sarah and her tennis. We couldn't even go out when Mom was waiting for Sarah's post-match call. [No cell phones in 1987]

Later, in a conversation with Mom about my new boyfriend, Jeff, she confided in me that she used to lay awake worrying about how she would pay for my wedding. She said that now she no longer has to worry because I can pay for my own wedding. Jeff and I had only been dating for a couple of weeks.

During our time together, Mom also referred to my first summer in DC and said that Dad "cooked it up for me to spend the summer in Washington." She never knew that the summer in DC was all MY idea.

There is so much deep inside.

I talked on the phone with Jeff and a couple of close friends. Mom, who was nearby, remarked to Sarah that *"this must be why I don't have many friends—I wouldn't want to have to call them."*

My friends are very important to me and I am grateful that I have such good friends.

Sarah returned the day before I was to fly back to DC and despite everything that happened during my visit, I wrote:

What a nice day and special evening with my family.

When things didn't go smoothly with Mom, I thought more about how much I missed Dad.

I miss Dad so much. It is so painful even when I am happy.

Jeff cared about me in a way I had not experienced in a very long time. He cared about whatever I was thinking or feeling. When I was sick with a bad cold, he said he wanted to see me, take care of me, and make me chicken soup. Though I wasn't feeling well, I had a hard time accepting care.

I really wasn't feeling well, but I feel guilty complaining about a bad cold.

In law school, much of December is spent studying for and taking comprehensive first semester exams under the pressure of knowing that the grade on the exam is the grade for the course. Jeff and I studied well together, and I always made time for a run.

> *I enjoyed my run so much, saw a beautiful sunset, and it was so good for thinking and clearing my head.*

I thoroughly enjoyed visits at Steve and Patti's house, even during exams.

> *It was a perfect afternoon. I felt so happy, content, and relaxed. With good music in the background and a fire in the fireplace, Steve read the paper, Patti read her book, and I studied.*

Mom was kind to send a card wishing me luck on my exams. Her gesture meant much to me. But on the last day of studying for my last exam, I was thinking about Dad.

> *I wanted to talk to Dad so badly, just pick up the phone and dial 312-280-6701. I still remember the number. It is so painful not being able to talk to him.*

When my first semester of law school ended, I was greeted with flowers from Steve and Patti. The card read:

> *Congratulations! You made it! We are very proud of you.*
> *Love Steve & Patti.*

As for me:

> *I started crying. I was on an emotional roller coaster feeling every emotion combined with being absolutely drained and exhausted.*

With some free time before the holidays, I went downtown and visited the law firm where I had worked. I felt proud to be able to say I had successfully completed my first semester of law school.

I spent lots of time talking to everyone. They are so nice to me and make me feel so welcome and cared about. It's a special place.

I spent the Christmas holidays with Mom and Sarah but then drove up to Rhode Island to ring in 1988 with Jeff, his brother, and his brother's girl-friend who, decades later, is my very special sister-in-law. Jeff's parents were away with his younger two brothers, but I met his aunt and uncle and both of his grandmothers. I would have loved more time alone with Jeff, but it was important to him that I meet his family members.

My last journal entry of 1987 reflected on a year of change. This had been my first year without Dad, I had left my secure law firm job, started law school, and had fallen in love.

I start 1988 feeling happy and secure with so much in my life having fallen into place. I am so grateful for the happiness I feel these days. I think I have come a long way.

Yet, in my long car ride back to DC, just after the new year, I had time to think and as usual my thoughts focused on Dad and how much I missed him.

Last year at this time I was so depressed, now I feel so happy. I feel guilty and scared that something will go wrong. I know I shouldn't think so much. I should just enjoy being happy.

Back in DC, with time to shop before the start of second semester, I still could not buy myself anything without feeling guilty.

I bought myself a pair of new pants. I feel so guilty. I feel like I am a bad person compared to how I used to be.

By mid-January, I felt I had never left law school. Our Property and Civil Procedure classes continued second semester, but Torts and Contracts were replaced by Criminal Law and Constitutional Law. I was back in the routine being with my friend between classes and hanging with Jeff as much as possible off campus. Though back into study mode, I always made time for my friends and exercise.

One day in Property, I heard: "Miss Epstein, the facts." Despite having been well prepared for class, I got one of the facts mixed up as I nervously responded to my professor.

I felt so stupid. It wasn't a big deal, but I just wanted to run away. I hate feeling stupid.

I was pleased with my first semester grades. I had worked hard, studied conscientiously, and prepared diligently for my classes. In law school, however, I no longer had the "Type A" personality that I had back in high school.

Sometimes I don't like my attitude. I want to get my work done rather than give it the perfectionistic focus that success requires.

I loved it when good friends visited from out of town. One weekend that winter, my roommate and I welcomed a mutual good friend from Brown, a former tennis teammate. We had fun together in DC and also loved relaxing in the apartment talking for hours about anything and everything. We were definitely moving beyond the mindset of our college years.

Part of me was psyched about going to a bar and staying out late, but the other side of me felt like that era was definitely over in my life. I am now so mellow, barely drink at all, and can't just let go and be all carefree.

I don't think I was completely carefree at any stage of my life.

These female friendships were important, however, and I went on to be a bridesmaid in both of their weddings and they were bridesmaids in mine.

Jeff and I were together as often as we could even when studying. For fun and relaxation, we went out to dinner, saw movies, or relaxed at my apartment watching television. On Thursday nights, we enjoyed pizza from a restaurant on the first floor of my apartment building. We would then study until *LA Law* came on at 10:00 p.m.

I love Jeff and I love being a couple. I think my love is growing stronger each day.

One Friday afternoon when I should have been enjoying feeling happy and relaxed at the end of another week, I got *"into trouble"* as Jeff would say. I started reading one of my Dad's books, "How to survive the loss of a love."

> *I started crying and crying. Why? I was so upset and feeling so guilty. I should be happy and relaxed on a Friday afternoon. Nothing is wrong but there I was crying my eyes out. I felt scared. I hate losing control. I feel like a bad person by getting upset when I have so much to be grateful for.*

Looking back, with the wisdom of age, experience, and years of therapy, I feel deeply sorry for myself at that time. I had never been given permission to feel emotions, especially negative ones. I thought being strong meant always being positive. I was filled with emotions, grieving the loss of my Dad, but had no understanding of grief nor how important it was to let myself feel those difficult feelings. Though I was happy on the outside, any time alone allowed space for those emotions to rise to the surface.

> *I like my alone time but when I'm alone, I think too much and get sad.*

Though Jeff would have preferred that I not keep a diary or *"secret life"* as he called it, I had no intention of giving up writing in my diary. I expressed its purpose at the beginning of a new volume.

> *Here is another piece of me—my thoughts, feelings, and the details of my daily life.*

As Jeff and I became closer, I let him read the parts of my diary about Dad's death. We had deep conversations about death and love, and "it made law school seem inconsequential."

> *I must feel so close to Jeff—no one reads my diary.*

For our four-month anniversary, Jeff surprised me with theatre tickets. He had to tell me in advance because Mom was expecting me to attend

Sarah's tournament in New Jersey the same weekend as the show. I had to tell Mom I would not be joining them. Even though I expressed it is terms of how thoughtful Jeff had been to surprise me with theatre tickets, Mom's response was *"You know where I would like you to be."*

I reminded myself that she only wanted me to come so that I could chauffer them around.

During spring break in March of 1988, Jeff and I went away for the weekend together. Our destination was Williamsburg, Virginia, a two-and-a-half-hour drive from Washington. We enjoyed being together away from the demands of law school. We took a horse and carriage ride around the historic area, explored the buildings from colonial times, ate at good restaurants, and didn't even mind that our motel was somewhat disappointing. This was a quick but perfect first getaway.

It sure was a wonderful trip together, hopefully the first of many.

The following week, Sarah turned 18 on March 17, St. Patrick's Day. I called to say a quick hello in the morning before she left for school with plans to speak again in the evening. When I called back, Mom clearly stated that I should not be disturbing Sarah during her homework time. If there were emoji's back then, I would have chosen the face with eyes rolling. Mom was so rigid and kept Sarah tightly in her bubble, even on her 18th birthday.

One of the biggest milestones during the second semester of first year law school is the writing of a brief followed by an oral argument. We learned how to write a legal brief in our legal methods class, but the assignment required significant research. One of the benefits of attending law school in the nation's capital was having access to the esteemed Library of Congress located adjacent to the United States Supreme Court. Jeff, my good friend from law school, and I spent hours at the Library of Congress doing research for our assigned briefs. Following successful completion of this hallmark legal writing assignment, there was the nerve-wracking experience of presenting our oral argument to our Legal Methods professor and answering her pointed questions derived from the brief.

Upon completion of the First Year Brief and subsequent oral argument, I felt a huge sense of relief.

I feel a sense of accomplishment having gotten this far through first
year. I think Dad would be proud of me.

Learning that I received an A on my oral argument made me so happy, I
cried.

I know Dad would give me the positive reinforcement I greatly need.

My journal at this time continued to reveal the seeds of an eating disorder
that had not yet bloomed.

At a restaurant lunch I had a salad so I could eat lots of breadsticks.

Though always a conscientious student, I couldn't pass up a social opportunity with good friends.

I should study but it sounded like fun. There was nothing I absolutely
had to do. Where did all my discipline go?

Before our attention turned to preparing for final exams, the law school
held its annual formal dance at a beautiful downtown hotel. The Barrister's
Ball, as it was called, was a fun, romantic evening, the event of the year! Jeff
looked handsome in his tuxedo and I wore a new black and white party dress
I had gone shopping for with my good friend from law school. She and her
boyfriend and Jeff and I had a very special evening socializing and dancing.

I love dancing with Jeff. While dancing a slow one, I imagined we were
dancing the first dance at our wedding.

Mom actually called to see how the Ball was. I appreciated her call. She
seems to be taking more interest in my life which is what I want so desperately.

This was early April of 1988 and Jeff and I had been a couple for five
months.

We are so close.

Like all new couples we had issues to discuss and resolve. Jeff had always expressed a desire for me to be more open, let my guard down, and express whatever was on my mind. I had gradually revealed more and had let Jeff read some poignant journal entries. He was patient when I got into one of my moods or started to cry but I sensed he wanted to know more about what was inside.

> *I talked a little bit about how I can't totally let go because I'm scared if I love too much and lose, then I will be hurt. I love Jeff so much but sometimes it's hard juggling everything.*

The final weeks of the semester increased the normal stress level exponentially.

> *Tonight, I was on the verge of a stress attack, but I caught myself by telling myself to only worry about one thing at a time.*

Professors were trying to cover as much material as possible and as students, we had to begin reviewing and studying an entire semester's worth of cases and concepts while also making sure we were prepared for the remaining weeks of classes. It was easy to feel overwhelmed.

> *So much coming up. I've got to take things one day at a time, so I don't get overwhelmed. I'm trying so hard to avoid stressing out.*

During those final weeks of classes, with semester exams looming, I was excited to accept an offer for a summer job at the American Psychological Association's Office of Legal and Regulatory Affairs.

> *The job sounds perfect—too good to be true. The work combines my interests in law, psychology, and health. It is well-paid, flexible, and in a great downtown location.*

I called Mom to tell her about my summer job opportunity and how I feel scared when things go well. She reassured me and gave me sage advice, "We should enjoy our blessings."

Around this time, Sarah was accepted by Princeton University. Upon getting this great news, I cried tears of joy. Then the tears turned to sadness thinking about Sarah's high school graduation without Dad's presence, and only I will care.

That same spring, Jeff's parents came to Washington, DC for a visit. I was nervous meeting them for the first time.

I'm so relieved. The first time is over and they like me. I like them too; they are just very different from my family.

May 1988 brought final exams and the end of my first year of law school.

I want to talk to Dad right now. I realize how fortunate I am to have people in my life who love me and support me. I can't feel sorry for myself for not having a Dad. I just hope though that he can look down and see me in my life. I try to make him proud.

Mom and Sarah sent a package to congratulate me on finishing my first year of law school.

They said they were proud of me and love me so much. That meant more to me than anything. I called Mom to thank her for being proud of me.

A few days after the conclusion of the semester, my Criminal Law Professor (no email back then!) called me. Why would a professor be calling me?! I was surprised to learn that I had received one of the highest grades in his class and he was offering me a research position for the summer.

I couldn't believe this was happening.

I felt honored but politely had to decline since I had already lined up a summer job at the American Psychological Association.

Before starting my summer job, however, I had the opportunity to take three major trips. The first trip was a solo road trip to Chicago, my first visit back since Dad's death. I had always loved to drive since I first got my license at the age of 16, but this would be my longest road trip, about 13 hours in my 1987 Volkswagen Jetta. There was no better way to unwind and clear my head after finishing my first year of law school. I drove 10 hours the first day, spending the night at a hotel in western Ohio. The next day, I was in Chicago by lunch time.

Driving west made me think about how when Mom and Dad upset me, I thought about getting in my car and just driving away.

Though I felt like that's what I was doing, this time alone in the car was not an escape but rather time for me, time to listen to cassette tapes (including one that Jeff had made for me), and time to think and reflect about Dad, law school, Washington, Chicago, and the special people in my life.

As I arrived in Chicago, I saw "my Lake" and followed the familiar Lake Shore Drive to Diana's condo.

I imagined that I was going to visit Dad—that he would be there to greet me.

I had a wonderful week in Chicago. It was a perfect combination of time with Diana, an evening out with a friend from college and time to myself which I always treasure. Each morning after Diana left for work, I ate breakfast at my favorite spot looking out at the Lake. I went for long runs along the Lake, through the Zoo, and along the magnificent mile, Chicago's shopping district. I toured the Art Institute and did some shopping.

But the primary reason for my trip was to go through Dad's belongings. When Diana was at work during the day, I surrounded myself with Dad's things. I cried so hard.

Delving into Dad's past makes me feel love and hate at the same time. He was so successful professionally, but his personal life was really fucked up at times.

For the trip home, my car was packed full with many of Dad's possessions.

Letters, pictures, mementos, clothes. What an adventure. I can't believe I drove all the way there.

After my trip to Chicago, I wasn't home for long before heading to Providence for Brown graduation weekend. As always, I felt great to be back, not only to see my friends but also to join Jeff and his family for his brother's Brown graduation.

In early June, I started my summer job at the American Psychological Association. My assignments involved researching legal issues that pertained to psychologists. I spent much of my time at the law library.

I loved my job at the law firm, but it is now so fulfilling doing work that is substantive. But every experience in my life has its place in my life along with its tremendous value.

The summer of 1988 was also Sarah's high school graduation in Rochester.

Rochester here I come. I've been waiting for this day for so long. I held back tears as I got closer. It's so emotional for me.

As usual, my time in Rochester was a roller coaster of emotions. Sarah's graduation and related events were very special, and I loved being back at Allendale Columbia and having conversations with former teachers.

I felt pretty and thin in my new outfit.

Sarah and I played tennis a few times and we loved having that time for just the two of us to talk.

I told Sarah I love her more than anything in the world.

I wished that I did not let things bother me when I was in Rochester, but it was hard, for instance, not having privacy to talk to Jeff.

When Jeff called, we were about to go to sleep. Mom didn't hear the phone ring but I did. I was scared Mom would be mad if I talked too long. I love Jeff so much and really wanted to talk to him.

It bothered me that Mom still controlled all food and drink. After tennis, Mom gave Sarah and me a drink.

I wonder what would happen if I just went into the kitchen and helped myself.

Another time after tennis, Mom made Sarah eat a full lunch, though she wasn't that hungry yet.

I just had grapes and milk having had a big breakfast. Mom thinks I am really negligent about eating and that I will corrupt Sarah.

Still, I enjoyed being in Rochester to celebrate Sarah's graduation from high school.

Tomorrow I'll be back to my Washington life which I love so much. Part of me loves it here. It's hard to bridge my two worlds.

I learned a lot during my time at APA that summer of 1988 and thoroughly enjoyed my usual summer fun in Washington, DC with Jeff and friends. My roommate for the past year moved home to her native Minnesota and my good friend from law school became my new roommate. I had plenty of time for fun on summer weekends, but Jeff would often be busy with Law Review assignments after a full week working in a law firm. We enjoyed whatever time we had.

I feel guilty sometimes for feeling happy.

Yet I also felt guilty for feeling sad.

I feel guilty getting upset about Dad when there is nothing in my life right now to get upset about. I feel like such a bad person when I get sad.

I wish I could go back and tell myself that I was grieving and that even when things are going well, the waves of grief can knock one over.

In addition to guilt, when I was both happy and sad, I seemed to have more thoughts about food and body image.

I wish I could eat without rationalizing it and feeling so guilty.

One of my tennis buddies said I looked "*thin and very good.*"

He told me I looked thin and that made me feel good. I must really have lost weight. He's not the first to tell me.

Even the building maintenance man said one day in the elevator that I had lost weight. Reading that in my journal so many years later, my first reaction was how creepy that an apartment maintenance man was commenting on my weight.

One day that summer I weighed myself on a scale in a department store. The number on the scale, even fully clothed, confirmed that I definitely had lost weight. I have no memory of needing to lose weight, but clearly "feeling thin" made me feel good about myself.

Perhaps this was my way of coping with my feelings of guilt; another seed of my eating disorder that was more than 20 years away from a full bloom.

I still loved any time I could get with Steve and Patti. They were happily expecting their first child, and I was excited for them.

Steve and I can really talk about everything. What a special friendship.

In August, I returned to Rochester as Mom and Sarah would soon move from the townhouse into a two-bedroom apartment where I would no longer have a bedroom. Though my room in the townhouse was much smaller than the bedroom I grew up in, at least my furniture was still there. I guess I wanted to sleep in my childhood canopy bed one last time.

I wish I could take my furniture back to DC so I would have something from my childhood bedroom.

I also was reunited with my childhood dollhouse that was packed away in the corner of the basement. Mom was ready to discard it in preparation for the move, but I needed to see it one last time.

> *Seeing my doll house up close after all these years brought back many memories of the innocence of childhood. I was in my own little world when I played in my dollhouse.*

While I would never see the doll house again, I carefully packed each piece of furniture in tissue paper and put it all in a box to bring back to Washington. Had I not been there, Mom would have thrown it away.

At the beginning of my stay, Mom seemed happy and relaxed and I was happy to be there. But by the end, the emotions were too much to bear. It started when Mom was in one of her over-sensitive moods.

> *I guess in Rochester I am just grasping for something that doesn't exist.*

While I have no independent memory of what caused Mom's over-sensitivity that day, I certainly remember its aftermath and ensuing emotional breakdown.

> *I love my family but sometimes the situation drives me crazy. I am only human for sometimes wanting things to be a way they never will be.*

That night I cried myself to sleep.

> *My last night in my childhood bed, and Mom didn't even say good night to me. It was so hard, and I couldn't even call Jeff or Steve.*

The next morning, I was packed and ready to go. I wanted to just slip out the door but Mom always said opening the front door might wake up Sarah.

> *I got the silent treatment until Mom exploded. All I wanted to do was get out of there and head back to my real home. Mom accused me of*

belittling her and acting as an earth-appointed Dad telling her how
to run her life. I finally left, still crying. Poor Sarah. I got into my car
free at last. My sunglasses hid my red eyes.

I cried almost the entire seven hours back to Washington, DC. I called Steve from a payphone along the way.

It was all so emotionally deep. I had many thoughts and flashbacks
from my life. I cried and cried.

Until this point, I had returned to Rochester each time with the hope that I would receive the unconditional love I craved. This trip drove home the reality that home was no longer with Mom but rather with me wherever I was. The emotions were overwhelming and I felt I was a bad person for having feelings.

It's hard not to acknowledge them when they are cutting at your heart.
Family problems are so emotional.

I wrote Mom a letter expressing some of the things I wanted to say but I struggled with being able to say what I really felt versus saying what she wanted to hear. No matter how much she hurt me, I could never drive a permanent wedge between us.

I can't be completely happy unless things are good between Mom and
me.

—

CHAPTER VIII

Law School:
The Second and Third Years

My second year of law school began with the confidence of a successful first year under my belt. While there were still some required classes such as Criminal Procedure and Evidence, I was also able to choose classes that interested me, such as Education Law and Juvenile Law. My living arrangement with my law school friend worked well, and Jeff and I were together as often as our busy schedules would allow.

Jeff surprised me with a party at his apartment to celebrate my 25th birthday. I felt so loved and still have the sapphire heart necklace Jeff presented to me that evening.

Over Labor Day weekend, Jeff and I enjoyed a getaway to Nags Head on the Outer Banks of North Carolina. As in Williamsburg, our hotel was far from luxurious.

We joked about how some day we will laugh about how we used to have to stay at motels like this.

Jeff and I had a great time, focusing on us and our relationship, eating well, and savoring the beautiful beaches and sand dunes.

We were both so happy and relaxed just walking along the beach. Jeff said he was falling in love with me all over again.

This was a perfect weekend to end the summer before the pace of second year of law school accelerated.

I feel very happy and in control these days. I get scared when things go so well.

Despite the emotional turmoil during my August visit to Rochester, I returned in September in a rented station wagon to drive Mom, Sarah, and Sarah's belongings to Princeton University. I helped Sarah settle into her freshman year dorm and I'll never know how Mom would have managed had I not taken a few days to ensure the move-in process went smoothly.

After saying our goodbyes to Sarah, Mom returned with me to Washington to spend a few days. I had invited her well before the August incident. My intention was to ease her transition to her empty nest to which she would be returning. Having been a full time mom for so long and having literally lived through us, I genuinely was worried about her being alone. Mom entertained herself while I was in class. Jeff and I surprised her with tickets to a show at the Kennedy Center.

Mom said she really likes Jeff. That makes me feel good.

Mom had hurt me so deeply only a month before yet, here I was worrying about her going home to an empty nest.

I called Mom to see how she was doing. She said she is doing great. What a relief.

Concerned with Mom's happiness, I also wanted nothing more than for Sarah to be happy during her first semester of college. It was as if I could not be happy unless Mom and Sarah were happy too.

I feel so happy knowing so many people are so happy. I am happy Mom is happy and I want so much for Sarah to be happy.

Anything less than happy would have caused deep anxiety for me. I thought a lot about Dad and how proud he would have been of Sarah at Princeton.

I hope Dad knows what Sarah is up to—he would be so proud of her.

During time alone, I often continued to look through Dad's memorabilia or read through diaries from the time of his death. The outcome was always the same, a good cry.

Tonight, I had a good cry. I guess every once in a while, I have a little "episode" to get some emotions out of me. I feel so guilty when I get like that because I am so happy with everything in my life.

As busy second year law students, Jeff and I did not get much time together. In addition to our full course loads, I worked part-time for APA and Jeff was extra busy with Law Review responsibilities. I admired Jeff for being so studious. Sometimes when he was studying or working long hours, I would feel guilty for being content with my efforts. I was conscientious but always made time for my friends and relaxing on my own.

I just know what makes me happy deep down and I have to be secure with that.

The end of October marked two years since Dad's death. I expressed to Steve how I felt I couldn't talk about it anymore because it had been two years. Steve said I can't keep it all inside.

I am so grateful for our friendship. Steve gives me a sense of security that I get only from him.

The time when Jeff and I could be together was extra special. On Thursday evenings we shared a pizza and watched our favorite drama about life in a law firm, *LA Law,* and on weekends we spent as much time as possible together including studying.

> *Our time together is so precious. I am grateful to have a man as special as Jeff. I hope we can have a long life together. I am so in love and it feels great.*

Mom and Sarah came to Washington for Thanksgiving 1988, which for the first time I planned to cook.

> *At the grocery store, I enjoyed picking out all the items for my Thanksgiving dinner. I hope it works out. I hope Mom and Sarah will be happy.*

Before Jeff headed home to Rhode Island to celebrate Thanksgiving with his family, he spent an evening with us.

> *Mom said things that drove me crazy. I feel guilty and like such a bad person expressing these things but if I don't, I'll go crazy. Dad sure had a lot of insight. But I love Mom so much, I shouldn't make a big deal about the things that bother me.*

Before Mom and Sarah's arrival, I thoroughly cleaned my apartment and car inside and out. I wanted everything for their visit to be perfect.

> *I hope I am not still grasping at something that doesn't exist.*

I put care and energy into making others happy yet whenever I felt happy it seemed to always be accompanied by guilt and fear that something bad was going to happen. So much anxiety beneath it all.

> *I feel guilty sometimes for feeling happy. I try to please too many people at once and it gets complicated.*

During final exam period, a very happy event diminished my motivation to study hard. Steve and Patti became parents for the first time when Patti gave birth to a healthy baby boy. I was ecstatic when Steve called me from the hospital with the exciting news.

> *It's hard to think about studying right now. Where is my motivation? With one exam to go, I went to the hospital to visit Patti and meet baby Sam for the very first time. He was so cute. I could have stared at him for hours.*

Once Patti and baby Sam came home from the hospital, I was able to hold Sam. I loved how Steve and Patti referred to me as "Aunt Betsy."

> *I love Steve and Patti and now Sam too!*

After the last exam of the semester, I was officially half-way through law school. I loved the holiday season and enjoyed shopping, writing out Christmas cards, and wrapping gifts. Jeff and I also had free and relaxing time together before he headed home to Rhode Island.

> *I am so happy when I am with Jeff. I like all this time we are spending together.*

Mom, Sarah, and I spent a cozy Christmas together in my apartment. Sarah and I had fun baking frosted Christmas cookies. We cut out Christmas themed shapes from the dough, and, once baked, we decorated them with frosting and red and green sprinkles. It made a huge mess which felt great in my own apartment. Mom never let us bake cookies like this when we were growing up as she did not want a mess in her kitchen.

After the holidays, I had more free time before the start of second semester. I loved being in my apartment cozily making scrapbooks and getting organized.

> *I love feeling organized.*

The time off from school had been wonderful but the motivation I lacked at the end of the semester remained.

As soon as this vacation is over, I better get my motivation back.

I not only had lots of reading to do for the start of classes, but I also seemed to be lax about my usually regular exercise.

I should have gone for a run, but I didn't. And I should have read but instead I organized pictures.

Unfortunately, evidence of a brewing eating disorder continued, which was not surprising given what I know now about the importance of expressing feelings, especially the difficult, painful ones.

For dinner I had salad and an orange. I finished up the M&M's, but I shouldn't have.

On a movie night out with Jeff, dinner was popcorn and diet coke. And one evening when Jeff wanted to get pizza for dinner:

I didn't want to eat pizza because I hadn't exercised, so I went up to the gym to ride the exercise bike. Then we enjoyed pizza together.

And yet another dinner at my apartment.

Jeff made his dinner and I ate some veggies and fruit.

I still experienced anxiety around doctor's appointments.

I hope my doctor's appointment involves no bad news. I hope I'm in good health.

Upon getting a good report:

I'm healthy—what a relief. I'm so grateful.

Day in and day out, I carried within me deep anxiety and a roller coaster of emotions.

Fortunately, my motivation returned and I resumed my conscientious ways second semester. I also got back into running which always felt good, not only because it was for exercise, but also because it helped me clear my head and relieve stress.

Mom came for a visit in February of 1989. Around my class schedule, I planned fun activities for us to do together including attending a professional women's tennis tournament that was in town. I was glad that Mom and Jeff could spend some time together too.

> *I glad Mom came. It was fun and good for our relationship but there is still that subtle tension. To even think about it digs so deep and brings tears to my eyes. I can't deal with having a confrontation with Mom. I guess I'll just keep things inside me.*

After her departure, I felt happy and comforted to be with Jeff and a run made me feel better too.

Overall, I liked my law school life. I was learning a lot and was managing my time well. I loved any time with Steve, Patti, and baby Sam. Jeff and I were together as much as possible, but he did not have the same work-life balance that was important to me.

> *Jeff has a hard time relaxing and hanging out and has so much on his mind.*

Our relationship was strong, and we were very much in love. We had more and more conversations about our future.

> *It's so flattering that Jeff thinks I'm sexy and beautiful. I've never thought of myself that way.*

I still had many episodes of being emotional and cried myself to sleep at times. I viewed the emotional side of me as a weakness and I felt I owed an apology to Jeff.

I told Jeff I was sorry for being in such a dependent and emotional mood instead of being my strong and independent self. Jeff was so loving and said it makes him feel needed.

For spring break that year we traveled to both Rhode Island and Rochester to visit our families. We were on the road for many hours, but a week together away from school was so good. It was hard having to stay in a motel in my hometown, but Mom now lived in a two-bedroom apartment and Sarah was also home for her spring break.

I think Mom was trying hard, but I still felt that she loves Sarah more and that we were interfering in her life.

Jeff remembers this first trip to Rochester for the March ice storm which had encased my car in ice. Jeff had to painstakingly chisel a thick layer of ice off the entire car—locks, doors, windows and windshield.

April brought the home stretch of second year of law school. On what would have been Dad's 59th birthday, I wrote him a card to express my thoughts. As I wrote, tears filled my eyes.

I'm crying and I don't know why. Maybe it's to relieve stress. No one really cares anyway.

In the birthday card, I expressed how much I wished he could meet Jeff.

He is a very special person who has added so much to my life in such a short time. I feel happy, loved and secure but it really hurts me that you can't meet him.

I ended the card's long note by letting Dad know that not a day goes by that I don't think about him and miss him.

*I hope you are resting peacefully with God. Thanks for being my Dad.
I will never forget you and everything you have done for me.*

A few weeks later I completed my second year of law school.

*I can't believe I am a third year law student. It's such a great feeling to
know I have worked hard and now I can relax.*

An important event at the end of the law school year was the Law Review
Banquet where Jeff was named Managing Editor, a huge honor. I attended as
his girlfriend and felt so proud of him.

*I am just so proud of Jeff and all he has accomplished. Where did my
ambition go? I'm happy and that's what counts.*

Jeff and I had had deep conversations about my former competitive self
and about how now it was important for me to do whatever I could to avoid
stress. We also talked about my fear of failure instilled in me long ago by
Mom.

Many entries in my journal continued to express tremendous guilt after
eating M&M's and another time, a piece of cake. I frequently had frozen
yogurt as my lunch. And there seemed to be a growing connection between
what I ate and whether I had gone for a run. I still thought of thin as a feeling.

I actually looked and felt thin in my charcoal gray pants.

The significant news that May was that Jeff and I had made the big decision to live together. We had been a couple for one-and-a-half-years. My
roommate was getting married that summer and would be finishing law
school in Pennsylvania. Jeff's busy schedule with classes and Law Review
limited the time we could be together. Living together made sense as becoming engaged was imminent and the timing was right. I did not know when we
would be engaged but needed to know it was definitely going to happen. In
my mind, that made living together acceptable. I had Mom's approval which
still was important to me.

Before beginning my second summer as a legal intern at the American Psychological Association, I travelled to Rhode Island for Brown's annual reunion/graduation weekend. Any time with Brown friends was special, especially a mini-reunion with my tennis teammates. Jeff also was in Rhode Island. I accompanied him to a family event but unfortunately felt as if I were coming down with something. I had no voice as I was introduced to relatives of Jeff's I had not yet met. Jeff flew back to Washington the next day to begin his summer job at a DC law firm. I, on the other hand, could barely lift my head off the pillow and spent the day in Jeff's twin size childhood bed sleeping off and on. Jeff's mother was kind, bringing me tissues and soup. Fortunately, my fever was gone the next day and I was able to drive home to Washington, DC.

Unfortunately, I had a lingering bad cough after I left Rhode Island. Patti gave me some cough medicine and Steve said he was worried about me.

Steve said I've gotten too thin. It means so much that they are concerned about me.

My next trip was to Princeton where Sarah had happily and successfully completed her freshman year. I helped her pack up and move out of her dorm. We were excited because after a few weeks at home in Rochester, Sarah planned to come to Washington, DC for eight weeks of her summer. We both eagerly anticipated her DC adventure.

Upon my return, Jeff had settled into our apartment.

It's exciting having Jeff here. I feel so happy though I'll be happier when my health returns.

It took many weeks to recover fully from the virus that set in when I was in Rhode Island. Fortunately, I eventually recovered without seeing a doctor. Steve and Patti continued to comment on my weight and a few people at my office asked if I had lost weight.

Everyone seems to be noticing. I hope nothing is wrong with me.

Sarah loved her time in Washington. We played tennis together and had lots of time to talk and hangout. We commiserated about Mom. She had made Sarah take a cab by herself to the airport for her flight to Washington.

> *I pray to God for forgiveness for the hostility I feel towards Mom. It makes me feel like such a bad person.*

In July, Jeff and I headed to Rochester to attend our law school friend's wedding in a nearby town south of my hometown. Before we left for this trip, Mom said that Jeff and I would have to stay in a motel even though Sarah was in DC. Jeff could have had Sarah's room and I could have slept in Mom's extra bed.

> *I am so angry and hurt. Mom can't be flexible for two nights! As usual, I didn't tell her how I feel.*

I had just stayed at the Brenner home and felt so welcome and cared about when I was sick, and Mom had no good reason why we couldn't stay in her apartment. I wrote Mom a nasty letter expressing my feelings. I never sent it. Instead, I stuck it in the back of my journal.

> *Jeff isn't stupid. He can figure out that you don't want him there. I thought you could be flexible for two nights. I treasure your visits and do everything I possibly can to make sure everything is perfect for you.*

My letter went on to express how deeply Mom had hurt me. If only I had been able to express my feelings to her rather than internalizing them and sticking the written version in the back of my journal.

> *I feel sad that Rochester can't be home to me anymore. Last August I went "home" searching for something I finally realized doesn't exist. I left heartbroken. I always thought of home as the place where I could always go and feel welcome. I don't know anyone else in their early 20s who had to leave home with every single one of their possessions.*

I will never know what would have happened had I sent that letter. As Jeff is typing this chapter, he says sending the letter would not have made a difference.

The rest of the summer was wonderful, working at APA, playing tennis, being with Jeff, Sarah, and friends, and being free on the weekends.

It's so nice to come home to Jeff. I tell him things I would have told my journal.

Jeff and I often met for lunch downtown during our work-days because even though we now lived together, Jeff spent many evenings at the Law Review office after a long workday. I loved when we were both home in the apartment.

I was glad to see Jeff relaxing.

During time together, Jeff and I were starting to have wedding-related conversations. Sometimes it was fun.

Jeff and I made lists of who we would invite to our wedding. I can't wait for the real planning to begin.

Other times it was more serious, such as conversations regarding our religious differences.

I don't want Jeff to give up and not want to marry me but I can't be someone I'm not. We love each other so much.

I eventually was able to tell Mom in a phone conversation how much she had hurt me. Mom said she thought about suicide when I first went to Washington.

The whole conversation hurt so much. I can't believe I actually opened up to her. I was crying so hard. Jeff was there and gave me a big hug. I felt guilty and good at the same time, yet I feel like such a bad person.

Much to my relief, in our next phone call, Mom didn't seem mad at me.

I feel better. I hate it when things aren't perfect between Mom and me.

Sarah, Jeff, and I spent wonderful time together that summer of 1989. Jeff was a good "big brother" to Sarah and she and I were closer than ever.

I didn't want to say goodbye to Sarah. In a way, I was jealous that she can still go home for a month. I know that I can never do that.

My summer as a legal intern at APA came to an end in early August. On my final day, my boss said that I was very thorough, that I thought clearly, and that I wrote very well. He also said that I was very conscientious and one of the nicest people he had ever met. He said he wanted me to be more "feisty," to bring my tennis mentality to my work. I appreciated his kind words, especially because at times that summer, I didn't feel fully motivated.

Jeff and I took a New England vacation as soon as we were both done with our summer jobs. After a visit with Jeff's family, we went to Cape Cod to explore and relax together. We even found the Lighthouse Inn where I had vacationed with my family as a young girl.

I felt so much inside being back there.

This break was just what we needed as our third and final year of law school was fast approaching.

I really like New England and I feel more and more comfortable at Jeff's house.

My journal, which had been my faithful companion for many years did not join us on our trip.

I didn't bring my diary on our trip because I am trying to wind down my journal writing. Now that I live with Jeff, it's harder to write on a daily basis. I'm getting to a new stage in my life—totally intertwined

with the man I love. From now on I will have the memories inside me
and will express my feelings to Jeff.

Many years would pass before I kept a journal again. My years of journaling provided great insight and understanding of myself.

Later in August, we started our third year of law school. Jeff and I felt settled in our life together, sharing our apartment and talking more and more about the future. Had we not been living together, being together would have been difficult given Jeff's Law Review responsibilities as Managing Editor in addition to our law school course load.

Classes this year included many electives in addition to classes that were strongly recommended in preparation for the Bar Exam. My favorite class that semester was an elective called Law, Science, and Medicine. Our casebook, as our textbooks were called, made reference to Dad's United States Supreme Court case in 1986. How I wished I could tell him.

Two weeks into our final year of law school, Jeff and I enjoyed dinner at one of our favorite restaurants in Georgetown. After dinner, Jeff suggested that we walk over to the Kennedy Center nearby. The evening was beautiful and the John F. Kennedy Center for the Performing Arts had a top floor outdoor terrace that wrapped around the entire building providing magnificent views of our nation's capital. The sun was setting when Jeff and I reached the terrace. He seemed a bit nervous as he reached into his pocket. Next thing I knew he was down on one knee asking me to marry him. The setting was perfect as Jeff placed his great grandmother's diamond in a beautiful new ring on my finger. I happily said yes! The date was August 31, 1989 and we were engaged to be married! We went to Steve and Patti's house to share our big news. They toasted us with champagne.

The next morning, I awoke to a birthday surprise. Jeff asked me to pack an overnight bag. Two and a half hours later we were at a beautiful resort to celebrate our engagement and my 26th birthday. The resort was by far the nicest place we had ever stayed. We had a wonderful time away from law school and city life. We had great meals, enjoyed the resort's amenities, and explored Charlottesville. This getaway was quick but perfect. We also made many phone calls sharing our big news with family and friends. Everyone was happy for us.

Every time I looked at the beautiful ring on my finger, it put a smile on my face. We needed, however, to focus on law school with our classes, studying, and planning for post-law school life.

A big part of the third year of law school involved interviewing in the legal world for after the Bar Exam. For us, third year was not only about the job search, but also the planning of our wedding. To say this was a busy time was quite an understatement. It was no easy task.

The easy part was sharing our happy news with family and friends. In October, Steve and Patti kindly and generously hosted an engagement party in our honor at their home. Jeff's parents and Mom and Sarah joined our Washington friends for the celebration. This was a wonderful evening filled with special people in our lives.

Mom seemed genuinely happy for us but never offered help with the wedding planning and she had already clearly stated that she would not contribute financially. At that time, traditionally many weddings took place in the bride's hometown, but I did not consider that as an option for me, due to Mom's lack of interest in hosting or planning. My mother-in-law would have loved us to choose a Rhode Island setting for a wedding, but that also was not an option since I was unwilling to yield complete control to her.

As busy third year law students, it made sense for us to get married locally. We were planning our own wedding and I was paying for it with money Dad had left me, so a Washington, DC area wedding was our first big decision.

When Mom was in town for the October Engagement Party, she said she did want to pay for my wedding dress. We went to a recommended bridal shop in nearby Alexandria, Virginia, and on the rack, I found the dress of my dreams. I appreciated this gift from Mom and the time with her to select my wedding dress.

Planning a wedding was very different in 1989. There was no internet for researching potential venues and all the associated wedding vendors. Instead, the arrangements involved many phone calls, brochures, and leg work. I loved to feel organized so I prepared a large binder with folders for the wedding planning details, venue, food, invitations, and photographer, to name just a few. Organization and attention to detail were essential, especially without a mother's interest, help, and input. In addition, I created monthly "to do" lists on large index cards. I loved the feeling of crossing out each task as it was completed.

We set the date for August 26, 1990, at the Hyatt Regency Hotel in nearby Bethesda, Maryland, only 10 minutes from our apartment. In addition to my binder which quickly filled with brochures and business cards, I also kept a notebook in which I wrote the details of phone calls, visits, and decisions. I chose pink and green as our wedding colors and even chose a pink spiral notebook and pink and green pens to use for recording the wedding details. My experience with weddings was minimal and here I was, planning one.

Jeff and I discussed virtually everything and even watched a performance of a band we were considering for our wedding. Patti had exquisite taste with everything and was a huge help with advice and recommendations pertaining to many of the wedding details.

Our life at this point revolved around law school and wedding planning. Mom and Sarah came for both Thanksgiving and Christmas. Jeff's mother had always booked his plane tickets early, assuming that Jeff would be home for all holidays. Jeff did go home to Rhode Island for Thanksgiving but, in 1989, he celebrated his very first Christmas with Mom, Sarah, and me. Having Jeff with us was wonderful, providing an opportunity to introduce him to some of our favorite Christmas traditions.

Jeff had been raised in an observant Jewish home. He attended his local Temple with his family for all Jewish holidays and celebrated each holiday with a big meal attended by extended family. Jeff celebrated his Bar Mitzvah, the Jewish coming of age at 13, and attended Jewish summer camp. He always envisioned getting married in a Temple followed by a reception with Jewish traditions.

When he met me, with the last name "Epstein," he logically assumed that I was a "nice Jewish girl from New York." The reality was that though Dad was Jewish and there were Jewish relatives going far back in Mom's lineage, I was not raised Jewish and knew very little about Judaism. My Dad was not an observant or practicing Jew and my Mom considered herself Christian, attending Protestant churches in high school and college. Though her father came from a Jewish family, he was a philosopher and an atheist, with no interest in practicing any organized religion. Mom's mother was a woman of faith whose favorite place to pray was New York City's famed St. Patrick's Cathedral. She had instilled her faith in Mom without any backdrop of organized religion. Both of my parents celebrated Christmas as children, and I developed my own faith in God as described in chapter three. My faith was similar to that of Mom and Grandma Bess; a strong faith, prayer but without an organized place of worship.

The differences in our religious backgrounds made wedding planning extremely challenging at times. I was a pleaser and wanted everyone to feel comfortable and be happy. If my parents had been at the helm guiding the planning, it may have been easier, but without that, my future mother-in-law felt it was her prerogative to step in and try to dictate certain aspects of the planning. On a trip to Rhode Island, I was literally interrogated by their family Rabbi to find out whether I was "Jewish enough" or would I have to convert to Judaism. I thought my agreement to be married by a Rabbi should have been enough. I was willing to do that for Jeff, but I did not appreciate his Mom's meddling to such a significant extent. I believed the fact that I was of Jewish heritage should have been sufficient, rather than being subject to a barrage of questions about my background.

Many aspects of wedding planning were wonderful. I chose pink and green floral print dresses for my bridesmaids, chose the stationery, enjoyed menu planning, food and cake testing, and with Jeff decided on the band, photographer, and videographer. We registered for gifts and picked out our china pattern.

As for invitations, we chose traditional ivory with black cursive engraved writing. As the one planning and paying for the wedding, it could be assumed that no parents' names would be on the invitation. Mom, however, felt differently. She provided no input or assistance with planning, yet insisted that her name be on the invitation "*or it will look as if you are an orphan.*" Instead of pushing back as I had every right to do, I assented to her request.

Mrs. Alice Denonn Epstein requests the honour of your presence...

Another major issue of contention was the guest list. While Jeff and I happily made lists of whom we each wanted to invite during our engagement weekend in Charlottesville, Jeff's mother, with no consideration for the fact that I was paying for the wedding, gave me a typed multi-page list of what seemed like everyone she had ever known. Jeff did have a large extended family and his parents had many friends, but her list was so much longer than my own list which included far more friends than family. Eventually, the Brenner list was pared down and they agreed to pay for some of the extra people they insisted on inviting. I never did receive that money though Jeff's parents generously hosted our rehearsal dinner and paid for our wonderful honeymoon trip to Bermuda.

In addition to the myriad of wedding planning details, our final semester of law school was about completing the requirements for graduation, signing up for the Bar Exam, and securing that first post-law school job. We had decided that we would either stay in Washington or move to Rhode Island. Jeff had said he eventually wanted to return to his home state of Rhode Island. For me, I knew the longer I stayed in Washington, the harder it would be to leave. The decision was made for us when Jeff was offered a one-year Judicial Clerkship in Providence to begin in September 1990. At least we would be moving to a place I was familiar with having spent my college years there. Leaving Washington was also made easier by the fact that Steve and Patti, who were expecting their second child, were contemplating an eventual move to Albany, New York, where Steve was born and raised.

In May of 1990, our graduation day arrived. Mom and Sarah were there for this milestone event as were Jeff's parents, brothers, and some members of his extended family. The only one missing was Dad, but I believed he was looking down on me from heaven with a huge smile across his face. Jeff and I received our Juris Doctorate degrees at Constitution Hall in downtown Washington. This was followed by a reception for the graduates and their families and friends on the American University campus.

We had a combined family celebratory dinner at the restaurant where we would be having our rehearsal dinner in a few short months. Steve and Patti were there to celebrate with me along with Mom, Sarah, and Jeff's family. Without Steve and Patti's love, encouragement, and support, I would have not made it through those difficult years following Dad's death, as well as the stressful times in law school.

But here I was a law school graduate now with a JD after my name. I had reached this milestone because of Dad and he was there with me in spirit.

My law school years were a time of tremendous personal growth and intellectual challenge. If there were a theme song, it would have been the Beatles classic, *I get by with a little help from my friends.*

The day immediately following our celebratory graduation day marked the start of our intensive Bar Review classes and the beginning of two months of full time preparation for the Bar Exam. Our only real break was a quick Memorial Day weekend trip to Rhode Island to attend my five-year Brown University reunion and for an engagement party hosted by Jeff's parents at their home. I had no family there but was pleased my Brown friends could attend the party.

Then back to our apartment to study day in and day out for week after week until the two-day Bar Examination scheduled at the end of July. Though we studied in Washington, we would be taking the Rhode Island Bar Exam, seeking licensure in the state where we would begin our married life later in the summer.

My first Christmas, December 25, 1963.

Six month portrait, March 1964.

Innocence of early childhood, 1965.

Devoted big sister to Sarah,
born March 17, 1970.

*Trip to the US Open at Forest Hills
ignited my passion for tennis.*

Tennis became a big part of my life, mid-1970s.

Proudly adding to my trophy shelf.

Allendale Columbia Graduation, June 1981.

Christmas 1981 with Mom, Sarah and grandparents.

Mom always made birthdays special.

Rare family picture, May 1985.

Time with Dad, Washington, D.C. 1985.

Brown University Graduation, May 1985.   *With my boyfriend, Jeff Brenner, Summer 1988.*

*American University Law School
graduation, May 1990.*

Our wedding, August 26, 1990.

Rhode Island Bar swearing in, November 1990.

Motherhood! Rebecca was born August 17, 1993.

Our family of three, 1997.

Celebrating a year of smiles—the twins'
first birthday, May 29, 2003.

Rebecca's high school graduation, June 2011.

Celebrating my 50th birthday on
Cape Cod, September 1, 2013.

Sharing my recovery story, November 1, 2018.

Vacation tennis.   *One of my favorite roles, Barrington*
                                        High School Tennis Coach.

Rebecca and Brandon's wedding weekend, June 2019.

Alexis and Matthew's high school graduation, June 2020.

The pandemic 2020.

CHAPTER IX

———

Marriage

After two solid months of studying, Jeff and I took the grueling two-day Rhode Island Bar Exam in Providence at the end of July 1990. Following the Bar Exam, we relaxed for a day at one of Rhode Island's beautiful beaches before focusing on our next task. We needed to find an apartment because we would not return until our moving day in September. Without the internet to check out possible apartments online, we scoured apartment rentals in the Providence newspaper, made appointments, and went in person to explore the possibilities.

We were fortunate to find a new one-bedroom apartment in a recently built apartment complex in Warwick, Rhode Island, about 20 minutes south of Providence. The complex was still under construction, so we were able to get a good deal on our rent. After three years of high rise living, we would now be on the first floor. We were excited that the apartment complex had a gym and swimming pool, but best of all, we would have our very own washer and dryer in our apartment. This was a luxury after years of saving quarters and sharing laundry facilities with other tenants. We secured our September move in date before heading back to Washington.

Before Jeff and I could focus solely on last-minute details of our wedding, we each attended the weddings of close college friends, Jeff's on Long Island, and mine in Minneapolis.

Our final pre-wedding events took place shortly after returning from our friends' weddings. Jeff's brother Rick, his best man, had a bachelor party for him and I had a special night out with Sarah, my maid of honor, and my bridesmaids.

The weekend of our wedding, I stayed with Mom and Sarah at the hotel where Jeff and I were getting married and Jeff stayed there too with his family. Jeff's parents hosted a wonderful rehearsal dinner for us at one of our favorite DC restaurants followed by a dessert reception at the hotel for the out of town guests.

The night before our wedding, I wrote Mom a note thanking her for my wedding gown and the special time we had together shopping for it.

> *Your first born is about to get married, but remember you are not losing a daughter, you are gaining a son. I will always need my Mom-me. I love you.*

From this note to her, one would think that we had a special mother-daughter relationship. I was an expert in trying to please her and tell her what she wanted to hear. Despite insisting that her name be on our invitation, she did absolutely nothing to act as a host during our wedding weekend.

On Sunday, August 26, 1990, at about noon, I was escorted down the aisle by Steve. We would later dance a special dance to *That's What Friends Are For*. The ceremony itself was performed by the Rabbi who had interrogated me months earlier in Jeff's parents' kitchen. It was important to Jeff's family that this Rabbi, who was also their good friend, perform our wedding ceremony. He had known Jeff virtually his whole life and that was evident in the Rabbi's words during the ceremony. For me, the only important and meaningful part of the ceremony was that Jeff and I were officially husband and wife.

After a cocktail hour, the reception began next door in the hotel ballroom. The wedding party was introduced and then *"for the first time as husband and wife, Betsy and Jeff Brenner."* We danced our first dance to Taylor Dayne's *I'll Always Love You*. Our best man, Rick, and maid of honor, Sarah, gave us beautiful toasts. Our guests danced the afternoon away to the music of our outstanding band. Of course, there were breaks for a sit-down meal and the cake cutting. The reception, after a year of planning, was a tremendous success. It was all over by late afternoon. I went out for frozen yogurt with Jeff while still wearing my wedding gown!

Jeff and I spent a fabulous week honeymooning in Bermuda where the biggest decision each day was beach or pool and which restaurant for dinner. We had been going non-stop and the honeymoon was a chance to unwind and relax. It was truly paradise and exactly what we needed after the Bar Exam and our wedding. I celebrated my 27th birthday with a horse and carriage ride in Bermuda.

Four days after our return from Bermuda we left DC with a 15-foot rental truck filled to capacity and my Volkswagen Jetta. We felt sad saying goodbye to Steve and Patti. They presented us with beautiful dress watches engraved with "Forever More." They said they were proud of us and would always be there for us.

Jeff soon began his Judicial Clerkship and I began my job search. During our first fall of married life, we travelled to Brooklyn, New York, seven out of eight weekends. Grandma Bess's health was rapidly declining, and she could no longer live independently even with home health nurses. What should have been Mom's responsibility quickly became ours. We made all of the necessary arrangements to move Grandma to a nursing home near us and cleared out the apartment that my grandparents had lived in for many decades.

Mom flew in only when we were selling Grandma's expensive furniture. Mom was in desperate need for cash and would accept any offer, without negotiation, usually significantly below what the item was worth. I managed to salvage meaningful things with sentimental value such as a box of love letters and journals from my grandparents' trips to almost every country in the world. Mom did not care about anything that did not have a monetary value.

In November 1990, Jeff and I were sworn into the Rhode Island Bar in an official ceremony in the Rhode Island Supreme Court. Mom attended and joined the extended Brenner family at a celebratory lunch. She said she was proud of me.

In December 1990, I was hired as Risk Manager and In-House Attorney at a community hospital that was also a teaching hospital for Brown University

Medical School. I drove about half an hour each way to and from work. I loved my job from the start. I had my own office, an assistant next door, and reported directly to the Senior Vice President. He had sincere respect for me as a lawyer. I admired his intelligence and learned so much from him. My favorite area of healthcare law was the human side. I served on the Bioethics Committee which was charged with advising doctors, nurses, and families on such issues as end of life decision making. I loved discussing cases and addressing ethical dilemmas and legal issues. I learned that Dad was a leader in the field of Bioethics at the American Hospital Association. I wished that I could have talked to Dad about my job and all that I was learning and experiencing in healthcare law, a field in which he had been a trailblazer. I felt happy when I met lawyers who knew of Dad or who had actually met him.

Another big part of my job was providing in-house education on medical-legal issues important to the physicians, nurses, and other staff. I wrote hospital policies and spoke on issues such as confidentiality and informed consent. I was 27 years old and was amazed when the Physician-in-Chief, someone much older and wiser, asked me for legal advice.

Mom and Sarah came for our first Christmas in Rhode Island. Our wrapped gifts were around a chair on which sat our stockings. Jeff was not comfortable having a Christmas tree in our home early in our marriage. I happily served Christmas dinner on our beautiful new china.

At some point during this Christmas visit, Mom and I got into a heated discussion that continued past midnight. I do not remember what sparked the argument, but I will never forget Mom shouting at me in the presence of Jeff and Sarah: *"Your wedding day was the worst day of my life, even worse than the day I was diagnosed with breast cancer."* The proverbial knife went deeper into my heart. There was no place to escape in our tiny apartment, but I remember sobbing in the bedroom. How could a mother say that to her newlywed daughter?! Jeff comforted me.

In planning our wedding, I had been very conscious of making Mom feel comfortable while meeting all the expectations of Jeff's parents. Accommodating our religious differences was not easy, but I thought I did a good job making our wedding a beautiful, happy, and meaningful occasion. I tried hard to please everyone at the expense of some of my own preferences. Once again, Mom had hurt me very deeply and to this day I can't watch our wedding video or look through our wedding album without feeling that pain. At the time I didn't know what to do with the pain and simply internalized it as I always had.

Jeff and I went on with our lives, both working as lawyers and enjoying life as a young couple in Rhode Island. Jeff's brother Rick was in his final year of medical school in Providence and a good friend of mine from college lived and worked in Providence. Making new friends was a challenge as we were both working full time. Living about forty minutes from Jeff's family, his mother not only expected, but assumed, we would attend every single family event including Jewish holidays, birthdays, backyard barbeques for Mother's Day and Father's Day, to name just a few. Several years would pass before we would establish our own life and community. Though I had moved into Jeff's home state, Rhode Island was familiar and I liked it. I missed my friends in Washington, but I was ready to leave city life.

We travelled to friends' weddings out of town and visited Steve and Patti and other friends in Washington. We were happy when Steve and Patti and their two adorable children visited Providence where, ironically, Patti's family was from. In fact, Jeff and Patti knew many people in common. Sarah visited us during her spring break to celebrate her 21st birthday. Jeff and I enjoyed movies, theatre, and sporting events.

By the summer of 1991, we had saved enough money from living in the tiny apartment to begin looking for our first home. I used what remained from the money I inherited from Dad after paying for our wedding to put towards a down payment. This enabled us to obtain a mortgage and buy a small house that we could afford.

There were two towns in Rhode Island with a reputation for the best public school systems in the state and similar to the type of town where I had grown up. We narrowed our search to small houses in these two towns. Jeff's mother could not understand why we were not looking to settle down in the town where Jeff had grown up. She was even mailing us house listings in her neighborhood. In her mind, though Rhode Island was tiny, the towns we were looking at were so foreign to her that it was as if we were looking to move to California! It was important to Jeff and me to find our own community and establish ourselves and identity apart from the world of Jeff's childhood. Jeff's mother thought this meant Jeff disliked his childhood. We had to reassure her we were a young couple in Rhode Island establishing our own life and wanted a town with excellent public schools for our future children.

In October 1991, we moved into an adorable two-bedroom home in Barrington, Rhode Island. There were built-in bookshelves in both the master bedroom and living room, a small kitchen and dining area, and a second bedroom upstairs. There was no garage and a small backyard, but it was our home and far more spacious than our tiny apartment. Barrington was a wonderful town on Narragansett Bay and the Barrington River. Our street of small homes was a dead-end street where we could see beautiful sunsets overlooking the cove.

Jeff now was an associate in a small law firm in Providence and I continued work at the hospital. We joined the YMCA so that we could exercise in the gym there in the evening after work. Our new home was perfect for us and we welcomed family and friends for visits. Despite what had happened the previous Christmas, Mom and Sarah joined us once again. We spent Jewish holidays with Jeff's family but gradually felt more comfortable passing on some of the less important family gatherings. We were putting down roots in our own community. Jeff was a founding member of the Barrington Education Foundation in the summer of 1992 and was appointed to the town's Zoning Board later that fall. Although he worked long hours at the law firm, he was beginning to make a name for himself in our new town.

I had always said that I wanted to have my first child by the time I was 30, and in November 1992, ten months before my 30th birthday, we learned that we were expecting our first child. When the time was appropriate, we happily shared the news with our family and friends. Jeff was making my dreams come true, a happy marriage, a house in the suburbs, and in a matter of months, a baby. Jeff made me feel happy, loved, and secure.

Despite significant morning sickness in the first trimester, I had a healthy and uncomplicated pregnancy. As my belly grew, I loved wearing maternity clothes, many of which were Patti's, and had several nice outfits for work. Jeff and I would often meet in Providence for dinner after work to satisfy my cravings for shrimp cocktail and nachos.

As we prepared the nursery, we were grateful for wonderful hand-me-downs from Steve and Patti who were now living only three hours away in Albany. We were living paycheck to paycheck and happily accepted their generosity.

Mom wrote us a congratulatory note in which she said my calling to share the news of my pregnancy was *"one of the happiest messages of her life."* She added:

> *May your first born be as easy to raise and bring you as much joy as mine has.*

Though she was genuinely happy for us, we only saw Mom once during my entire pregnancy. In April 1993, Jeff and I travelled to Montreal for our last getaway as a couple. We then drove to Rochester to see Mom. I wanted her to see me pregnant. She was now working in retail and had very few days off. Her debt had been growing and she had to get a job. She resisted for so long because she felt working was beneath her. She no longer had money coming in from a family friend's company. They had been paying her to write the company newsletter. She had not been earning enough to pay her bills, so with each passing month her debt was compounding.

In May we drove to Washington where a baby shower was given in my honor in Sarah's apartment. After graduating from Princeton, she was working at a law firm in Washington and living in the same apartment building I had lived in during law school. Celebrating my pregnancy with my sister, sister-in-law, and very close friends, was very special. Jeff's brother, Rick and his wife were now also living in DC for his residency. In June, my mother-in-law graciously hosted a baby shower for me in Jeff's childhood home. There were many, many people there, but only a handful that I knew well. I had many more friends in Washington than I did in Rhode Island at that time.

I worked through the end of July before beginning my maternity leave. A group of friends from work surprised me with a wonderful baby shower at a local restaurant.

After a long, arduous 26-hour labor, we welcomed Rebecca Bussell Brenner into the world on August 17, 1993, at 3:45 a.m. She was thankfully healthy with a full head of brown hair. Jeff and I were feeling on top of the world, now a family of three. It was truly love at first sight as my dream of being a mom had come true.

In the weeks that followed, friends and family members visited us, excited to meet baby Rebecca. This was a very special time in our lives and we adjusted easily to parenthood. Rebecca was a happy baby, and slept through the night very early on.

For my 30th birthday, two weeks after Rebecca's birth, we went out to dinner at a nearby restaurant. Rebecca slept peacefully at my feet in her car seat/baby carrier throughout the meal. I had received the best possible 30th birthday gift, my precious baby Rebecca.

―――――

CHAPTER X

Motherhood

M om met Rebecca for the first time when she was six weeks old, having arranged consecutive days off from her retail job to travel to Rhode Island. I felt excited going to the airport to pick up Mom and introduce her to her granddaughter. It was love at first sight. I have a photograph of Mom holding Rebecca in her arms in a chair before we even left the airport. The look on Mom's face said it all. She was one happy Grandma and in love with baby Rebecca.

My maternity leave ended as the new year, 1994, began. As much as I loved my job, I loved being home with Rebecca more. There was no way we could afford to live on one income at that stage, but I was able to reduce my work hours to 20 hours a week. We were fortunate to have Rebecca cared for by our pediatrician's nanny, who was no longer needed full time for her children. The first morning, after an evening of tears, I went off to work in blizzard conditions. I felt welcomed back at the hospital, but I missed being at home with Rebecca. Fortunately, our nanny took wonderful care of Rebecca and left me detailed notes about everything that happened while I was at work.

Just a few months after returning to work and adjusting to being away from Rebecca 20 hours a week, our nanny announced that she had decided to move back to her home state of Wisconsin. The mere thought of finding a new nanny brought on tears. I couldn't go through the process of finding a new caregiver for Rebecca.

By this point, Jeff had received a small raise. We crunched the numbers over and over and concluded that I could stay home with Rebecca provided we were very careful financially. I would give tennis lessons on weekends to bring in extra cash.

I felt overjoyed, although giving notice and walking away from a job I loved would be difficult. My boss had other ideas. He wanted me to remain employed to work on projects from home and go to the hospital once a month to attend Bioethics Committee meetings and consults as needed. This perfect arrangement began in April 1994.

I loved being home with Rebecca. She was an absolute joy. We enjoyed long walks in the spring weather and had playdates with other moms and babies. Rebecca was a happy, playful, and curious baby. We did everything together from trips to the zoo to reading books at home. A family moved in next door with a little girl three months younger than Rebecca. We developed a close friendship and our neighbors became our first real friends in Barrington.

In April 1994, we took our first trip to Washington, DC as a family of three. This was a special time, introducing Rebecca to our friends there and visiting familiar spots.

Mom came for a Mother's Day visit in May 1994. I had sent Mom pictures of Rebecca since her October visit, and she sent monthly homemade cards. I filled her in on Rebecca's milestones as she reached them, sitting up, first tooth, crawling, and many more. On that Mother's Day weekend, Mom was very happy to have her second in person visit with her precious granddaughter and loved every minute of their time together. She joined us for Rebecca's first haircut and first pair of shoes. She left not knowing when she would be able to visit again.

She also left without disclosing that she was in a dire financial situation. She had reached her credit limit on multiple credit cards and continued to go into further debt each month since her meager retail paycheck did not cover her monthly expenses.

In a phone call several weeks later, Mom shared the big news that she would be leaving Rochester to live in Greenwich, Connecticut, with the family who had generously paid her for producing a monthly newsletter for their company. Mom was not happy about leaving Rochester after calling it home for over 30 years. But she felt she had no choice because of her financial situation. Her friend paid to store her furniture and move her to their enormous home in Connecticut. They travelled a lot and Mom went on an adventure to Utah with them. The new arrangement seemed to be going as well as possible, given the challenging circumstances.

In July 1994, about a month before Rebecca's first birthday, Mom literally landed on our doorstep. The family, who graciously took Mom in, could no longer tolerate Mom's OCD and rigidity. One morning I received a phone call from Mom's friend who said that Mom would be coming to us later that day. Mom arrived by train from Connecticut with her clothes and $5000 from her friend to start a new life in Rhode Island. There was no discussion; this situation was our reality.

Mom slept on the couch in our tiny house for a few weeks. Rebecca provided the only release of tension between us. I tried to be patient and supportive, but, as always, I suppressed my feelings within. I had to go to my closet to have any phone conversations about the situation. Jeff and I went for walks when he got home from work so I could debrief with him and give myself a mental and physical break from Mom.

Having hit rock bottom financially, Mom had no choice but to declare bankruptcy. Jeff represented her in the bankruptcy. As stressful as the situation was, I could not abandon her as she had her own mother.

The sooner we found Mom an apartment, the sooner she would be out from under our roof. With 11-month-old Rebecca strapped in the car seat in the back seat, Mom and I drove around to check out local apartments. We quickly found that an apartment complex was not an option because her bankruptcy status would prevent her from passing any credit check. We eventually found an apartment in the next town over. It was the first floor of a house owned by a local businessman. We could bypass the credit check by putting down both the first and last month's rent. It came out of the $5000 gift as did the money to purchase a used car for Mom. Mom's friend arranged for her furniture to be shipped from storage to her new apartment. Rebecca was perfectly behaved during this process of settling Mom into life in Rhode Island.

Mom's debt was eliminated by bankruptcy but she would need to work as soon as possible and live completely within her means. We were not in a position to help her financially, but I gave her the gift of my time and patience in handling every detail of this sudden and significant disruption in our lives.

Through connections in town, we found two part-time jobs for Mom. She would work four days a week in a local clothing store and both weekend days as the receptionist at a local real estate office. Working six days a week left her one day off—Wednesdays. With no washer and dryer in her apartment, Mom did her laundry at our house on Wednesdays. During that time, Mom gave her full attention to Rebecca. She loved being a grandma, reading books and sitting down on the floor to play with Rebecca and her toys.

Mom settled into her new life and work routine in Rhode Island. I worked on a limited basis from home, taught some tennis lessons, but most of all I treasured each day of being a full-time mom to Rebecca.

Mom joined Jeff's parents and our friends in celebrating Rebecca's first birthday less than a month after her abrupt arrival in Rhode Island. Mom's flexibility and resiliency was uncharacteristic, but she came down off her pedestal, was an excellent employee, lived within her means, and most importantly was a special grandma to Rebecca.

On Wednesdays when Rebecca saw grandma walking towards our front door, she would say "Ma" with excitement. Coming over to do her weekly laundry soon turned into spending the entire day with us. Rebecca adored her grandma Alice.

I was unable to be open and honest with Mom and tell her how deeply she had hurt me, but here she was living nearby, working in our community, and she actually seemed happy.

On Wednesdays, we did many things together beyond playing with Rebecca at home and occasional shopping. We went on long walks with Rebecca in her stroller and enjoyed day trips around Rhode Island and nearby Massachusetts.

Our life was all in the present, but I was starting to feel as if I had a mom. She even began to know Jeff better and appreciate what a great guy he was. Jeff often brought pizza home after work on Wednesdays and Mom usually stayed to join us for dinner.

With Mom living in Rhode Island, we celebrated holidays, birthdays, and everyday life together. For the first time in my adult life, Mom understood me and appreciated me and my life. Looking back, I wish we could have had honest, open conversations about the hurt from the past, but that was something I was not capable of doing. Mom joined us for Thanksgiving at Jeff's parents' house, and they made her feel very welcome.

At Christmastime, Mom put up a tree in her apartment and we went over to help decorate it. Having a Christmas tree once again meant a lot to me, and more so because we could share this tradition with Rebecca. Mom gave Rebecca a Sesame Street character ornament because Rebecca was passionate about all the characters from the quintessential children's show. This thoughtful gesture evolved into giving my children a new ornament each year reflecting an interest, activity, or milestone from the year. We went to Mom's apartment for present opening on Christmas morning and ate Christmas dinner at our house. Sarah came up from Washington, DC for our family Christmas celebration.

Mom loved giving back to us by babysitting for Rebecca from time to time such as when I had a meeting at the hospital or a tennis lesson to teach. She also would occasionally babysit in the evening so Jeff and I could enjoy a date night out.

Working six days a week, Mom was busy, but she was happy and at peace. While Wednesdays were always set aside for "Ma", Rebecca and I enjoyed many activities on the other days including story time at the library, playdates, trips to the mall, the zoo, and the playground. We were also happy playing at home both inside and outside with our good friends next door.

The real estate office where Mom worked was next to a small pond with a white gazebo and a few benches. During her lunch hour, Mom sat on one of the benches to eat her sandwich. Sometimes we would go see her there, and feed the ducks from the gazebo. Wood's Pond became Mom's favorite spot in town.

Our adorable first home was feeling very small as Rebecca grew into toddlerhood. We also hoped to have another baby. We needed more space but were limited in what we could afford. Two houses down from us, the family was building their dream house in a nearby town and needed to sell their existing home which was the biggest house on our street. There were three bedrooms, a big family room, a garage, and a big backyard. They offered us a great price and in November 1995, we moved two houses away, on the other side of our good friends next door.

We were excited to have significantly more space and two-year-old Rebecca adjusted easily to our new home, loving her new play area in the family room. Mom was a huge help as we settled in. She loved to clean and helped entertain Rebecca. We experienced many happy Wednesdays in our new house, and I can still picture Mom sitting on Rebecca's child-size pink chair to play with Rebecca in her dollhouse, her big second birthday gift from us.

Mom fit in well with the women realtors at the real estate office where she worked on weekends and they were very kind to her. Mom also enjoyed the office holiday party, and we enjoyed another wonderful Christmas at her apartment.

In January 1996, Mom turned 60. Wanting to make this milestone birthday special for her, I organized a surprise party for her at the real estate office. All her friends from the office were there along with Jeff, Rebecca, and me. Sarah was supposed to fly in, but bad weather cancelled her flight. Mom was completely surprised and felt deeply happy and cared about. She was showered with attention, gifts, and cake! It was a truly special celebration and I made her an album with pictures and mementos from her party.

On her actual birthday, Rebecca and I took mom out for a lobster lunch and presented her with a gold heart necklace. She loved the seafood, especially lobster, one would have thought she was a native New Englander! Rebecca wore the gold heart necklace on her wedding day in June 2019.

She adored her Grandma Alice, whether it was our Wednesday outings or babysitting in the evening.

Rebecca was anxious for us to go so she could have grandma to herself.

After a wonderful day together, Rebecca told grandma, "*You're my best grandma.*" Later she said she wanted Grandma to move her bed into our house and said, "*I love it when grandma comes over.*"

In May 1996, Mom took a flight and we drove to Washington, DC to attend Sarah's Law School graduation. This was a special time for our family. After the event, Mom flew home and we continued to Sesame Place in

Pennsylvania, a Sesame Street themed park. Rebecca loved seeing her favorite characters. In June, we travelled to Rochester for my 15th high school reunion. It was meaningful showing Rebecca where I grew up and she loved seeing my childhood home and school.

As Rebecca approached her third birthday in the summer of 1996, Mom happily helped me with the fun details of planning a circus-themed party. This was a wonderful project for our Wednesday threesome, going often to the local party store.

On a special Wednesday in late July, Mom, Rebecca, and I took a day trip to Cape Cod. I wanted Mom to see the Lighthouse Inn where we had spent delightful family summer vacations in the late 1960s and early 1970s. I loved being back there with Mom, now only 90 minutes from our Rhode Island homes.

The following weekend, Jeff, Rebecca, and I spent a wonderful weekend away only to learn upon our return home that Mom had a fall at work and could barely walk. It was the beginning of August 1996 and our lives were about to turn upside down.

CHAPTER XI

And Then She Was Gone

Mom was never one to rush to the doctor, so when she hurt her leg in a fall at work she insisted she would be fine after a few days of rest. We brought her to our house where she rested on our couch while Rebecca and I catered to her needs. Her job at the clothing store required that she be on her feet all day and now that was not possible. Each day out of work was a day without pay.

With no improvement after several days, I convinced Mom that she needed an x-ray. I took her to our local urgent care center which coincidentally operated under the auspices of the hospital where I had worked full time and now worked on a very limited basis. The urgent care center, after a preliminary reading of the x-rays, recommended an expedited review of the x-rays by the Radiology Department at the hospital. I took the x-rays there myself. With Mom waiting in the car, I proceeded to the Radiology Department where thankfully I was known by the Chief. He reviewed the x-rays himself. The news was both shocking and devastating. Mom had fractured her hip in the fall and the x-rays revealed evidence of metastatic disease.

She would be admitted to the hospital immediately and surgery to repair the fractured hip was scheduled for the next morning. Mom and I were sitting in the Admitting Office and the Clerk asked Mom for her insurance card. I knew she had reduced her coverage to catastrophic care only to save money, but I was speechless when Mom responded to the Clerk that she had no insurance. This was not the time to lecture her about letting her insurance lapse as she was being admitted for surgery and evaluation of metastatic cancer shown in the x-rays.

Although she had no insurance, she was given a private room because the nurse manager on the floor knew she was my mother. When she was settled in, I left and went to Mom's apartment to gather her toiletries and other necessary items for her hospital stay.

I told Rebecca that Grandma was in the hospital to have an operation on her leg that she hurt when she fell. Rebecca talked to Grandma on the phone and always gave me messages to deliver to her Grandma. "Tell her I love her." Rebecca also made special pictures to hang on the bulletin board in Grandma's hospital room.

The surgery to repair Mom's fractured hip was successful, but the overall news was grim. Mom's breast cancer, first diagnosed 14 years earlier, had come back in virtually every bone in her body. The fall at work was a result of Mom's cancer-weakened bones, a pathological fracture.

I was in the recovery room with Mom after her surgery and stayed with her once back in her room. She was in relatively good spirits though at that point the focus was on recovering from the surgery.

The Chief of Oncology met with Mom early in her hospital stay. After several diagnostic scans, she received the devastating news that because the cancer was throughout her body, in her bones, and lesions elsewhere, chemotherapy was not an option.

Meanwhile at home, we were getting ready to celebrate Rebecca's third birthday. I had to explain to Rebecca that sometimes people have to miss special events that they were looking forward to attending. Rebecca was sad that Grandma could not come to her birthday party, but we assured her we would have another celebration when Grandma came home from the hospital.

Mom's hospital stay extended from days to weeks. She struggled with the physical therapy that was necessary for regaining the ability to walk on her surgically repaired hip. She had to cope at the same time with the reality that her cancer was untreatable and every scan or test seemed to reveal a new lesion. Cancer in the bones is extremely painful so strong narcotics were prescribed. Mom expressed concern with developing an addiction to narcotics, though at this stage comfort was the priority. She lived by the mantra of one day at a time, even one minute at a time. She was not ready to face her mortality.

A few weeks after her third birthday, Rebecca started nursery school at the Barrington Early Childhood Center. Rebecca loved school and we both made many new friends.

I visited Mom in the hospital every day. Rebecca was either with a friend and a friend's mother at our house or theirs. On weekends, Jeff and Rebecca had fun father-daughter time. I drove half an hour each way to the hospital and stayed for about an hour. I brought Mom her favorite cheese on raisin bread sandwiches and vanilla cream cookies. I delivered her newspaper and mail daily and took care of anything that needed to be done. I rarely could just sit by the bedside as Mom's daughter. I talked to her health care providers, paid her bills, and communicated her condition to others.

When I wasn't there, Mom did crossword puzzles, watched television, and read the newspaper. The nurses were attentive and the oncologists were caring and made time to sit by Mom's bedside during their rounds. The social workers tried to help Mom cope with her terminal condition, but Mom maintained her reserved demeanor and would not open up to them.

Mom's cancer was vicious. When a lesion was found on her spine, they rushed her by ambulance for emergency radiation treatment at a nearby Radiation Oncology facility. I followed in my car and waited in the waiting area until her return trip to the hospital.

Mom had a high level of pain tolerance but eventually she had no choice but to give in to the excruciating pain and take narcotic pain killers. With cancer-weakened bones, spontaneous fractures are inevitable and Mom soon needed a cast on her right wrist, her dominant side. Seeing her becoming more incapacitated, unable to even hold the pen to do her crossword puzzles made me feel sad. She had been writing notes for me to bring home to Rebecca, but eventually Mom had little strength left to write, especially with her non-dominant left hand.

Mom talked to Rebecca on the phone but did not want Rebecca to come to the hospital and see her looking unwell. She had been in the hospital for about a month when I finally managed to convince Mom that Rebecca NEEDED to see her.

This afternoon I told Rebecca we were going to visit Grandma Alice and her face lit up. Grandma seemed happy to see her and had tears in her eyes.

This was the first of many visits and Rebecca always lifted Mom's spirits. She would bring a new picture for the bulletin board, sing her nursery school songs for Grandma and even show her a few steps learned in her weekly dance class. We would sometimes bring our lunch and eat with Grandma.

Mom's hospital stay was prolonged by the frequent discovery of new lesions as well as the lack of progress in physical therapy to learn to walk again. The day after a few steps were hesitantly taken, a new large lesion was found in her leg. Eventually, a lesion in her left wrist bone combined with the fracture in her right resulted in Mom being unable to use her hands.

By mid-October, the Oncology team explained to Mom that there was nothing more they could do for her. They had been very caring, sitting by her bedside and even brushing her hair when she was no longer able to do so herself. Once Mom was not followed by the Oncology team, she would hear their voices outside nearby rooms. She felt extremely hurt that they no longer even popped in to say a quick hello. They couldn't treat her cancer and had only hospice left to recommend. Mom felt abandoned and I felt sad for her though I understood that she was no longer an oncology patient, and the doctors had other cancer patients to care for.

Mom remained on the orthopedics surgical service only because she could not walk. The staff were strongly recommending that Mom enter a nursing home for rehab until she was considered safe to go home. By now, Mom had been in the hospital for two and a half months and was no longer in need of acute care. She wanted to come home to my house, but I was not a nurse; I was a lawyer, a mother of a three-year-old, and lived in a split-level house with many steps. Mom reluctantly agreed to be discharged to a nursing home.

She was unable to pay any of her hospital bill which was approaching $100,000. When the social worker came to Mom to help her apply for

Medicaid so the hospital would be paid something, Mom felt insulted. "*That's welfare*" she exclaimed. I had to explain to her that this was necessary because she had no health insurance. Inside, I wondered to myself, how could she have not maintained her catastrophic coverage.

Despite a body riddled with cancer and still unable to walk, Mom insisted on going home to her apartment against the medical advice of the nursing home. She refused any in-home services. Instead, she expected me to visit every morning, help her get out of bed, make her breakfast, and ensure she was settled in her chair. During the day, friends from the real estate office would come by with food and to visit. Two of them had first careers as nurses and would graciously help Mom to the bathroom. A new friend of mine, a nursery school mom, was a certified nursing assistant and helped Mom in the evenings.

This was a very stressful time. I tried to keep things as normal as possible for Rebecca with nursery school and ballet class and playdates. Rebecca was smarter than her three years. She asked many questions about dying and heaven. On her own, she came to the sad conclusion that her beloved Grandma Alice was not going to get better. Though Rebecca had adjusted well to nursery school, around this time she would cry at school and the teachers would have to call me. Rebecca was fine if I was there. She was sad about Grandma Alice but unable to express it. She did finally verbalize that she feared I would have to go to heaven too since my Dad was already there and my Mom would be going there soon. I reassured my sad little girl that I did not have to go to heaven too.

Within a few days of being at home, Mom called me to say she heard a crack while sitting in her chair. I had been trying to have a normal day with Rebecca and nursery school friends. We were about to go to "story time" at the Library. Instead, Rebecca stayed with our friends, and I left immediately to follow the ambulance with Mom inside back to the hospital emergency room. Another pathological fracture had occurred, this time while sitting in a chair. Mom was readmitted to the hospital.

Evaluation of the latest fracture revealed the aggressiveness of Mom's cancer. A spot was found on her lung as well, but Mom would not consent to an invasive biopsy. She was taking what remained of her life one hour at a time. It was time to face her mortality as she was discharged to yet another nursing home, this time with hospice care. It was early November of 1996, now three long, brutal months after Mom's fall at work.

After being spoiled with a private room in the hospital, Mom was now in a semi-private room with a woman in her 90s with advanced dementia. While this roommate was a typical nursing home resident, Mom was an alert, intelligent, 60-year-old living in a body taken over by fiercely invasive cancer. Rebecca had a hard time coping when I was out of her sight, but I visited Mom every day, now bringing her vanilla milkshakes, the only food that appealed to her.

The hospice team cared for Mom in an exemplary way no hospital medical team could ever do. The hospice team focused on Mom's emotional and spiritual needs, while also providing her with a more comfortable bed and advocating for more morphine to control the constant, unbearable pain. They gave her the personal attention and care she needed as she faced the cruel reality that her life on earth would soon end.

Rebecca was filled with many questions. Why do people get bad diseases? Why do people die? How do they get to heaven? So many worries for a three-year-old. I had to reassure her over and over that I did not have to join my Mom and Dad in heaven as she feared. Rebecca understood that Grandma would be living in the nursing home until she went to heaven.

One evening after dinner, Jeff, Rebecca, and I were in Mom's apartment packing up her things when Rebecca adamantly insisted that I take her to see Grandma for a quick hello. Tomorrow was not soon enough, she insisted on that night, so of course I took her. I think Rebecca needed reassurance that her beloved Grandma was still there.

A gifted hospice chaplain, Susan, was the only person with whom Mom truly connected during this horrific ordeal. Susan prayed with Mom, meditated with her, and helped her to feel God's love as the end of her life drew near. Mom's faith was as strong as ever as she faced her now certain mortality. A nurse's note in Mom's chart read:

I have no incentive. I'm just waiting for the end.

The nurse wrote that Mom had accepted the fact that she was going to die and hoped it would be soon.

I was grateful Mom had daily emotional and spiritual support from the hospice chaplain as well as daily visits from a very caring hospice nurse. As for me, I felt no emotions. The stress level was palpable, and adrenalin got me through each day. My energy was completely used up each day in attending to each day's details and being a full time Mom to Rebecca.

I did take time to reflect and made a memory book which I presented to Mom. I made lists of childhood memories under categories such as Tennis, Birthdays, Christmas and added recent categories such as Washington, DC and Rhode Island. On the first page, I wrote:

For my dearest mother—with love and gratitude

I prefaced the lists of memories with five written pages:

I hope this collection of memories and quotes brings a smile to your face.

I expressed in writing what I was unable to say face to face:

As I write, tears are streaming down my face, reflecting on the past and thinking of what you have so bravely endured since August. It pains me to see you suffering emotionally and physically. You are the most courageous woman I have ever met.

I thanked her for being such a special grandmother to Rebecca, giving her so much love, attention, and affection.

She will never forget you. Memories live forever. I will miss you so much and will feel a tremendous void.

I believed Mom's two years in Rhode Island were a gift from God, filled with precious days creating memories. I gave this special memory book to Mom. I know she read it privately, but I never witnessed her reaction, nor did we have any real conversations about it.

A few weeks into November, Mom needed increasing amounts of morphine to control the pain and thus slept more and more. She could no longer tolerate the vanilla milkshakes, but she got mad at me when I arrived one day without one.

Jeff, Rebecca, and I continued to go to Mom's apartment to pack things. It was strange knowing she was still alive, yet also knowing the harsh reality that she would never return there. She had made it her home in the midst of her financial crisis, and we had spent happy times there, especially at Christmas. We could not afford to pay the next month's rent so we had until the end of the month to finish packing.

By November 25, 1996, Sarah was with us, spending as much time as possible by Mom's bedside. Rebecca asked that afternoon to go to the nursing home, as I had told her that Grandma was going to die soon. We stayed only a few minutes

I knew it would be the last time Rebecca would see her. Grandma knew we were there, though she didn't speak. She waved her finger at Rebecca, and Rebecca blew her kisses.

On November 26, 1996, Rebecca had a good morning at nursery school and was delighted when both Aunt Sarah and I showed up for the goodbye song. At 3:15 that afternoon, Mom took her last breath. She was gone. I explained to Rebecca that Grandma's heart stopped beating and she was no longer breathing. She went to heaven. She was finally at peace.

I want to be a child forever. I don't want to ever die...

said my little girl.

The next day, the day before Thanksgiving, was spent meeting with the Hospice Chaplain, the Funeral Director, selecting both a casket and a cemetery plot. Susan, the Hospice Chaplain, kindly agreed to officiate at the funeral since Mom, who was working every weekend, had no place of worship in Rhode Island, thus no clergy who knew her.

On Thanksgiving Day, we went to Jeff's parents' house as was assumed and expected, despite the death of Mom two days earlier. At that time in my life, I always did what was expected of me. I was not capable of saying I needed a day at home. Sarah and her fiancé, who had flown to Rhode Island, joined us for the traditional Thanksgiving meal. They also spent time packing Mom's furniture into a rental truck for delivery to our house. We stored the furniture for them in our basement until they could take what they wanted to their townhouse outside Washington, DC.

Sarah and I also went through Mom's clothes, jewelry, pictures, and anything else with sentimental value. Time was of the essence. Already it was late-November, and we had to rush through this difficult process before the last day of the month.

That night, Rebecca seemed very sad though she wasn't expressing what she was thinking.

I just held her tight.

The next morning was the funeral. I had made the difficult, but age-appropriate decision that Rebecca would stay at our neighbor's house. I explained that the grown-ups were going to a service and the cemetery, but that Rebecca would join us later back at our house for what would seem like a party.

Susan led a beautiful service at a funeral home in nearby Bristol, Rhode Island. Mom's favorite songs *On Top of the World* by the Carpenters and *Younger Than Springtime* from the musical *South Pacific* were two of the musical selections. A simple casket covered in flowers sat at the front of the room. Steve and Patti interrupted their family Thanksgiving to fly in for the day. Many of Jeff's family members came as did several of Mom's friends from the real estate office. I was in no shape to speak so Jeff read from my memory book preface on my behalf.

> *My childhood is such a part of who I am today. Thank you for being such a devoted mother. Never did I feel that I came from a broken home. You provided us with a happy, secure, and loving home, a place to thrive. You protected us from a harsh world and from your own hurt. You gave us so much of yourself and made us feel special and loved. You set an example of motherly love and devotion, honesty, and integrity, values to live by. I love you, Mom. Thank you for the bottom of my heart for everything.*

Mom was buried in a Barrington cemetery located a few blocks from the town beach. Back at the house, Rebecca loved the attention of her aunts, uncles, and other special people in her life. I displayed a collage of pictures I made of Mom through the years. I had a large basket with individually wrapped slices of bread. A small hand-written note in front of the display stated one of Mom's favorite sayings and activities:

Take time to feed the ducks

Then it was over. Once the rituals of the death, funeral, and burial are done, loved ones and friends return to their homes and their lives. Jeff went back to work on Monday. Rebecca and I went back to our lives, but we were left with a huge void following Mom's death. Wednesdays were especially difficult.

The holiday season, usually a happy and festive time, was upon us. Grandma Alice had joined us the past two years for our annual visit to Santa at our local mall. This year, she was with us in spirit. Not a day went by that Rebecca didn't share some memory of her beloved Grandma. We went to Wood's Pond to feed the ducks where we felt both Mom's presence and absence. Rebecca even asked if the mailman could deliver mail to heaven for Grandma. I explained that the mailmen can't go there because they are still alive but that we can tell God anything that we want to tell Grandma. I was not in touch with my own emotions but very tuned into Rebecca's. Rebecca somehow sensed when I needed an extra hug or an "I love you Mommy."

The past two Christmases we had decorated a tree in Mom's apartment. Jeff had never had one in his own home. Now that Mom was gone, I wondered what would happen to this meaningful tradition that Jeff had now witnessed first-hand and he knew how important it was to me. We compromised on a small "memory tree" that fit perfectly in the large bay window in our living room.

Rebecca was so excited to put the ornaments on the tree. We got out the Santa Claus I made when I was three, Grandma's special ornaments, including Wood's Pond and Rebecca's Sesame Street ornaments.

Rebecca's new ornament this year were wooden pink ballet slippers.

Mom's tradition would continue! We placed an angel on the top of the tree. Rebecca and I now talked of Grandma Alice as an angel, so symbolically she was looking over us. The angel ornament at the top of the tree belonged to my parents, along with other angels that we hung near the top of the tree. Jeff was clearly out of his personal comfort zone, but he knew this tradition was important to Rebecca and me, and less than a month had passed since Mom's death.

That night in her prayers, Rebecca, through God, told Grandma Alice that we decorated the tree just how she would like it.

We put an angel on top of the tree because you are an angel.

That was a very special evening.

Unfortunately, Jeff's mother was neither understanding nor compassionate. Standing in our garage, she berated Jeff for having a Christmas tree in his home, specifically mentioning that just because Alice died it didn't mean we had to celebrate Christmas in our home. Here we were in our early thirties, adults with our own home and child, and she felt the need to try to dictate what Jeff should and should not do. My mother-in-law's insensitivity made me angry and I reassured Jeff how much I appreciated his letting Rebecca and me share in this special tradition and meaningful way of keeping Mom's memory alive.

Sarah, her fiancé, and his nine-year-old daughter from a previous marriage, joined us for Christmas. We said prayers before Christmas dinner and Rebecca spontaneously added *"please take care of Grandma Alice in heaven."*

The new year 1997 brought plenty of snow and the familiar routine of nursery school, ballet, play dates, and library story time. Jeff continued to work six or seven days a week. I focused on being the best Mom I could be. It was all about Rebecca. Where was all the hurt and pain from the past? Where was my grief? The pain and hurt were deep down inside, likely around the wound caused by the "knife" that went deep into my heart years ago. The feelings closer to the surface were feelings of gratitude from the two years I had with Mom in Rhode Island.

I was raised to be strong which I still thought meant focusing on the positive rather than acknowledging and feeling the difficult emotions. I was like a dam that could burst at any time. I believed that if I ever started to cry, I would be unable to stop. So, I went about my daily life "keeping it together" the best I could.

By March of 1997, Rebecca had more incidents at nursery school where she would start crying for no apparent reason. At home, she often acted out the hospital visits to Grandma Alice with her Barbie dolls. Rebecca's nursery school teacher said Rebecca was likely grieving and the tears were happening at school, the only place she was without me. For a few days I sat in the corner of the room at school and while I was there, Rebecca happily went about her routine. When I suggested leaving for a bit and coming back, Rebecca looked as if she would burst into tears. At home I got Rebecca to express that she missed Grandma and wished she could come back.

I arranged a meeting at our house with another member of the Hospice Team. Gwen, the Bereavement Chaplain, helped families get through the first year after the loss of a loved one. She came to our home one afternoon at my request to meet with my sad little girl. Gwen was wonderful. She read books with Rebecca and had her draw pictures of how she was feeling and pictures of things she liked to do with her Grandma. Rebecca drew a picture of herself sad with tears. Gwen said Rebecca's crying at school was normal grieving and we should continue doing what we are doing—looking through pictures, sharing memories, and talking about it all.

I was worried about my sad little girl, but Gwen sensed that I needed help too. I still didn't know how to grieve, but was about to embark on the most difficult but necessary journey of my life.

CHAPTER XII

———

My Grief Journey

M y grief journey took me places I did not know I needed to go. I had minimal experience with feeling difficult emotions. After Mom's death, I thought I was supposed to focus on the two good years I had with each of my parents before their untimely deaths. I certainly knew sadness, but I had no idea how to bring all of my feelings to the surface to confront and process them. I had deeply complicated relationships with both Mom and Dad. My grief for them was destined to be complicated too.

When Gwen, the Hospice Bereavement Chaplain, came to our house on a March afternoon, four months after Mom's death, my only concern was how to help Rebecca cope with her sadness. Gwen, however, sensed that I needed help too. She strongly encouraged me to speak to a counselor friend who specialized in grief and loss. My initial reaction was to ask, "What's wrong with me?" Gwen said she would accompany me if I didn't want to go alone, and I reluctantly agreed to go.

At 33, this was my first experience with a therapist. For the first time I had a safe place to begin to talk about my life—my parents' divorce, their deaths, and my relationship with them when they were alive. Unfortunately, I equated vulnerability with weakness, and kept my guard up. I answered the counselor's questions about my past and kept my appointments, but I avoided getting in touch with the feelings deep inside. I always felt the need to feel in control at all times. I felt guilty for being anything other than happy since I had a wonderful husband and daughter as well as a great life.

My problem was that I had never been allowed to feel. As a child, I felt guilty for having any negative thought. I believed being a good person meant always being positive, appreciating the good, and never expressing the bad. Focusing only on the two good years with Mom and Dad was delaying my grief.

After several sessions talking about my parents, the counselor termed the trauma my parents had inflicted on me as emotional abuse. I would literally need permission to feel if I were to begin to process the years of emotional abuse. Keeping it all inside and focusing on being a good mom to Rebecca seemed so much easier. I did not know then that being a good mom meant acknowledging all emotions, both happy and sad.

While Jeff, Rebecca, and I continued to enjoy life as a family of three, a persistent sadness in me wouldn't go away. At times, I felt as if I were just going through the motions. I constantly had what I described as an uptight feeling. Sometimes I felt rage which scared me or I felt on the verge of tears but could not cry. Other times I did cry, but only when I was alone.

Poet Robert Frost's words *the best way out is always through* applies to the grieving process. If my grief had been the proverbial elephant in the room, I was tiptoeing around it. Grief required that I lean into all the feelings which went against everything that was deeply ingrained in me from a young age.

In June 1997, seven months after her death, I wrote Mom "a letter" in which I expressed how I was feeling.

> *I can't even put into writing how I am really feeling. I know you would expect me to be strong and just go on. I am really having a hard time. Rebecca has been my escape and excuse for not confronting my feelings. It is catching up to me. I am filled with anxiety and at times it completely consumes me. I have been told I look very sad. The pain is so deep. I can't seem to bring it to the surface.*

Sarah walked herself down the aisle at her wedding that August of 1997. Though there was much tension between us, I was the matron of honor and gave an emotional toast at the reception. Sarah and I were grieving in very different ways. Sarah was happy Mom's pain and suffering were over and she focused on life in the present. I also focused on life in the present but with constant sadness and overwhelming emotions simmering beneath the surface.

My grief journey had barely begun when, after about a year of counseling sessions, my counselor informed me that she was returning to Ireland, her homeland. I was slowly but surely making progress, but now had another loss to contend with. She said I was doing good work but was not done yet. She and Gwen strongly recommended a skilled therapist they knew who saw clients in her waterfront home one town from me. The thought of starting over with someone new was unfathomable but with Gwen's involvement and urging, I decided to give this new therapist a try. I hated the word "therapy." I thought of it crudely as paying someone to pretend to care.

My sessions with the new therapist got off to an unsettling start when, at the first meeting, she asked if my parents were still living. I thought to myself, *doesn't she already know this?* However, Barbara was a warm, caring therapist and I soon felt comfortable going to her house. I eventually accepted that I needed this safe space to talk and continue what I had started. She would offer a cup of tea before I sat down and sometimes gave me a hug as I left.

We discussed difficult topics and I started to let my guard down enough to be able to express some of my complicated feelings. First and foremost on my mind, I felt deep regret that maybe I did not do enough for Mom at the end of her life. I feared that she died feeling abandoned because I didn't take her home with me. I needed to hear from Barbara that I was a good daughter during that difficult time. Despite Jeff's reassurance, I was wracked with feelings of guilt. Regret is a tough emotion in processing grief and for me it was an impediment to moving forward.

In another "letter" to Mom, I wrote:

> *I blame myself that your final weeks weren't spent in the comfort of home with me at your side holding your hand. One of my greatest fears is that you died disappointed in me. I keep feeling that I let you down.*

In addition to regret, I was burdened with guilt. I felt guilty for having thoughts or talking about the bad times with Mom. I felt guilty because of the pain she endured before she died and the depth of her suffering. My grief put Mom on a pedestal. I felt a huge void without her but delving into the pain inflicted before her move to Rhode Island was extremely difficult.

During this time, Jeff and I were trying to give Rebecca a sister or a brother. I hoped getting pregnant would ease the emotional pain. After invasive testing for both of us, there was no medical explanation for our inability to conceive, despite trying for several years. This added to my emotional upheaval. Looking back, I still had significant grief work to do. Now was not the right time for me to bring another child into the world.

In the aftermath of Mom's death, I had vivid dreams almost every night. Mom featured in each dream and the common theme was feeling that she did not care about me. Sometimes I would wake up crying after yet another nightmare. All of these dreams were documented in my journal, providing a reminder that I needed to work on all aspects of my complicated relationship with Mom, not just the happy times from her two years in Rhode Island. Mom indeed did suffer and endure severe pain at the end of her life, but the guilt I felt for talking about the bad times had to be set aside in order to address my own pain within.

I was able to put down on paper the essence of my complicated grief. Through therapy, I understood it intellectually, but remained unable to feel the difficult emotions and let them go. The pervasive sadness continued for several years. I felt like a "therapy failure" and though I recognized my need for a safe place to talk about difficult topics, I resisted vulnerability and dependency.

I want all the hurt to go away. I need for the hurt to go away and then
I can be left with the wonderful memories that fill my heart with joy.

I was suffering for having avoided confrontation. If only I could have told Mom how much she hurt me.

I hide emotional wounds that cannot seem to heal. I never learned
that it was okay to feel sad or express anger.

In my grief journey, I learned about my sad inner child, but did not learn how to nurture her and take care of her in a healing way.

There was, and still is, a little girl inside me who desperately needed her Mom. I needed to be loved, loved the way I love Rebecca. I still need that love to make up for all those years Dad chose to live 1,000 miles away and love for those years you were so distant, I need love to fill the huge void left by deaths of the ones who were supposed to love me unconditionally even into adulthood.

An old scrapbook reminded me that in my college dorm, I had a poster on the wall with a teddy bear that said *inside all of us is a child just wanting to be loved.* I was that child. Right now, my need was to be loved unconditionally, to feel that love and to have lots of TLC.

In my prayers at that time, I would pray that I was a good enough daughter and ask for forgiveness if I had let Mom down in any way.

A friend gave me a journal and told me to *open my heart and soul and feel what's inside.*

I feel really sad inside and feel so alone with my thoughts and feelings. I am hurting inside and need someone to care.

Yet, day to day, I lived my wonderful life with Jeff and Rebecca.

I'm so happy in my daily life and I have the best husband and daughter in the world. Why do I feel so troubled and unable to verbalize exactly how I feel? Why do I get so angry and sad?

The recurring theme throughout my grieving was feeling guilty for the sadness I felt because of the wonderful life I had. In my mind, pain and joy could not co-exist. At times, I would decide to "just be happy" yet each time the anxiety and sadness crept right back in.

Gwen came to my house for more bereavement sessions and had to reassure me each time that everything I was going through was normal grieving and that continuing the hard work I was doing in therapy, talking about the pain and sadness, was important. I felt comfortable talking to Gwen and greatly appreciated her reassurance and support.

Gwen always makes me feel better. I hope I don't lose her too.

Sadness, anger, anxiety, impatience, agitation, rage, and guilt ebbed and flowed, yet I somehow managed to keep it together. I only cried when alone, when Rebecca was asleep, and when Jeff was out at a meeting. Looking through old scrapbooks and diaries was triggering.

> *This afternoon I felt horrible—on the brink of emotional and physical exhaustion and collapse. I could have slept all afternoon but Jeff had to go to his office. He offered to stay home but I would have felt too guilty. I really don't know how to take care of myself. I pulled myself together.*

There were more signs of depression and it scared me.

> *Tonight, for some reason, all I wanted to do was get in bed and watch TV and escape from everything. I just felt so droopy and weepy inside and unable to articulate it.*

Evenings were the worst when I was alone.

> *Tonight, I just lost it. I can't even describe it. I was so upset. I cried a lot and just completely fell apart. I felt like I could go into a rage. I felt lousy.*

At this time, I was playing no tennis and have no recollection of excessive thoughts about food or exercise. I worked out at our local gym a few days a week while Rebecca was at nursery school.

> *I exercised at the YMCA today. It felt good physically, but I still feel in my "depressed" mode. I don't understand why I feel so down when I feel so happy with my life.*

I was frustrated feeling this way and constantly talking with my therapist not only about what I needed to do, but also how to actually do it.

I'm so scared and I don't want to lose control. I'm so good at keeping it together. There's so much inside me from the past, but I can't just unravel and fall apart, because I am so lucky to have a wonderful husband and special daughter.

My therapist said I needed to keep talking about everything and eventually the difficult emotions would come to the surface. I'm not sure they ever did, thus contributing to the development of a full blown eating disorder many years later.

It's so discouraging when I feel down. I just want to snap out of it. I am so happy yet there is so much sadness inside me—deep emotional wounds that aren't healing. I don't like feeling this way, but I can't get it out.

In 1998, I participated in the "Making Strides Against Breast Cancer Walk." I walked the five miles on a beautiful October day, hiding teary eyes behind my sunglasses. Many people walked as part of a team, but I walked alone.

I felt good when I finished though I had no one to share it with. Hopefully Mom was watching from heaven. I felt so alone.

I only seemed to be able to cry when completely alone.

Tonight, when Jeff was at his Zoning Board meeting, I cried and cried—so painful.

I clearly was grieving and did not know that all the crying was actually feeling the pain.

Tonight, I cried and cried while Jeff was at the YMCA. I worry that I am depressed. Jeff worries too.

Though living through it, I obviously knew very little about grief. I developed an intellectual curiosity and began to read everything I could about

grief and loss. My thirst for knowledge on this subject led me to serious edu-
cational books about grief and loss as well as simple, short books with advice
for coping with grief. Gwen said in one of our meetings, "I have plans for
you," but I had no idea what she meant.

   The term self-care was not in my vocabulary or even realm of understanding, yet I did two new things just for me. Early on Sunday mornings, I started
going on solo, 10-mile bike rides along the East Bay Bike Path to Colt State
Park, an expansive waterfront park on Narragansett Bay. Before reversing my
route and heading home, I would get off my bike, sit down on the rocks, and
just enjoy sitting quietly by the water.

> *I love sitting by the rocks at Colt State Park on a sunny Sunday morn-*
> *ing. It is so peaceful listening to the sound of the water hitting the rocks.*

   I also discovered a love for walking along the beach. Jeff, Rebecca, and I
took a short trip to the Lighthouse Inn on Cape Cod. Jeff said he hadn't seen
me so relaxed in a long time. The Lighthouse Inn was special because happy
childhood memories were attached to it—memories from when my family
was intact. To be there as an adult with my own family made me happy.

> *I went for a walk on the beach early in the morning and just couldn't*
> *get enough of life's beauty. It was so powerful, so spiritual—the sun-*
> *rise, the sea gulls, the ducks, the beach, the sound of the ocean, the*
> *quiet. I feel like I am really living again, not just going through the*
> *motions.*

   At my next session with Barbara, she asked a poignant question—*did I*
believe that I deserved to feel happy?

> *I drove to the beach and cried. I went to Mom's grave, not too far*
> *away, and spoke to her. I asked for a sign that it's okay to let go of my*
> *grief and the pain from the past.*

   I wanted permission to live and be happy and not be consumed by the
inner emotional turmoil that tormented and consumed me. I had to somehow

let go of the guilt and regrets. Looking back, I thought about how Mom had controlled and programmed me and how maybe I had been depressed off and on since high school. I always told Mom exactly what she wanted to hear and avoided confrontation at all cost.

The racing thoughts continued and Jeff thought I was deeply troubled. I wanted to get pregnant. I thought that would solve everything and we could proceed with our lives. The time still wasn't right.

My grief journey encompassed not only a search for inner peace, but also a spiritual journey. This journey had originated in my childhood when at times I craved organized religion. I had a strong faith, but I had never had a spiritual home. I had attended our town's Interfaith Thanksgiving Service, held each year in the week of the anniversary of Mom's death.

> *It was a very meaningful and beautiful way to honor Mom's memory. I felt such a connection to Mom and to God. Just being in a Church and singing hymns touches something deep inside me. It comforts me.*

I tried to explain to Jeff how I felt, but we were so different spiritually, and I didn't want anything to come between us.

> *I need religion and formal worship, but not Judaism. I tried but it is not for me spiritually. I need to do something for me. Jeff says I can go to church as long as Rebecca doesn't know.*

A few weeks later, I attended a Sunday service at the "White Church" as it was called. It was a quintessential New England Congregational Church.

> *I'm so glad I went. I loved the service and especially the sermon.*

In my therapy sessions, I was starting to understand how selfish Mom had been and that she must not have been a happy person.

> *I am grieving both a relationship that didn't exist in addition to the relationship we did have during the last two years to her life.*

Bike rides, beach walks, and Church helped me to find some peace amidst the sadness, and during these times of peace, my emotions could more easily rise to the surface.

Another important piece of my journey was something that Susan, the Hospice Chaplain, said during one of her visits. She said, "You don't have to wait for the pain to go away to help others." Her words were profound. I would not wake up one day to find the pain had suddenly gone, and I would be healed. The time was right to do some positive things, not only for me, but also for others.

I was thrilled when Gwen asked if I would participate on a panel with her and Susan along with a Hospice Physician and an Ethicist. We would be talking to a group of Brown Medical Students about death, dying, bereavement, and ethics.

*I am so excited that Gwen thought of me. It's exactly the type of thing
I'd like to do.*

It was a success and I felt good about myself after this incredibly positive experience.

*It was an exhilarating experience. I hope I have more opportunities. It
feels good to feel passionate about something.*

I began accompanying Gwen and Susan to events related to grief and loss. I felt increasingly more comfortable sharing my experience with others. Barbara's husband was the Executive Director, and Gwen was a Board member of an organization called Interfaith Healthcare Ministries. Next thing I knew, I was a new Board member. I met so many inspiring people; warm, kind, and spiritual individuals from different backgrounds, many of whom were clergy. The organization trained clergy and lay people in pastoral care and provided education on spirituality and health. I loved the monthly meetings and annual board retreat and conference. Once again, I was grateful to Gwen for providing this opportunity. I was starting to understand what she meant by "I have plans for you."

Susan trained me to become a certified hospice volunteer. I was able to visit and support hospice patients and help lead bereavement support groups.

My own experience with grief and loss was now helping others in need.

I continued to attend services at the Congregational Church on a regular basis. I had found my spiritual home and now had the spiritual nourishment I had always craved.

I loved my beach walks and, once again thanks to Gwen, began to collect sea glass. Jeff would join me when possible and we would take long relaxing walks on our town beach, collecting shells and sea glass. We were enjoying simple summer pleasures together.

Jeff gave me so much love and support following another fulfilling experience. The Barrington Clergy Association presented a four-part series on Spirituality and Health. I was honored to present Mom's story—one of pain and suffering and how faith helped her cope as she faced the end of her life.

It was a very special evening. Having the opportunity to share helps me heal.

I was excited to share the news with Sarah that Mom's story would be a case study for Interfaith Health Care Ministry's Annual Spirituality Conference. I also told her about becoming a hospice volunteer and getting involved with bereavement programs. Her reaction was that everything I was doing seemed depressing. For me this work was not depressing, but rather an important step forward in my grief journey.

During this time, Rebecca was a bright, happy elementary school student. I was very active in her school on the Executive Board of the Parent Teacher Organization, chairing school events and volunteering in the classroom. Rebecca loved school and enjoyed soccer, dance class, and girl scouts. We both made many new friends. While she was in school all day, I engaged in my own pursuits; workouts at the gym, coffee dates with friends, long walks, and meetings associated with Interfaith Health Care Ministries and Hospice. After school, my focus was on Rebecca, which made me happy and content.

I continued my weekly therapy sessions, which were necessary and invaluable, though I still viewed them as hurting my self-esteem and making me feel vulnerable. Vulnerability in my mind remained a negative, equated with weakness. I was in the infancy of learning about my needs and was unsure about how to meet them without experiencing tremendous guilt. I did not understand that this process was an essential piece of my healing. Dependency on this safe space to talk was enabling connection with deep-seated feelings that I desperately needed to uncover and confront.

The new millennium arrived with hope for the future and a new home. In April 2000, we moved a short distance to a four-bedroom colonial in a neighborhood filled with young families and a short walk to Rebecca's elementary school. This began a new chapter in our lives. Barbara stopped over with a big, beautiful shell, a simple housewarming gift with symbolic significance. She said the shell was a reminder of my inner strength. The only thing missing at this time was another baby.

Two symbols that took on great meaning in my life were ducks and stars. For some bereaved people it's butterflies or cardinals. For me it was ducks. Mom loved to sit by Wood's Pond and together with Rebecca, we would "take time to feed the ducks." After Mom's death, ducks showed up in unusual places. On the day of our move from the house in which Mom had spent much time, two ducks showed up at the end of the driveway. This was a first! I felt Mom's presence as if she were there remembering the good times we had shared in that house. Then, on Mother's Day 2001, two ducks appeared in our front yard. Again, I felt Mom was making her presence known. In the ensuing years, unusual duck sightings continued to happen from time to time. They still do.

When I look up at the stars on a dark, clear night, I feel Mom's presence. There is no time more profound than walking out of Church Christmas Eve after singing Mom's favorite carols. I walk to my car on the dark, clear night. I look up at the stars and she is with me.

The stars took on more meaning as I looked up to them and said to myself the familiar nursery rhyme, "*Star light, star bright I wish I may I wish I might have the wish I wish tonight.*" I had one wish . . . to become pregnant.

———

CHAPTER XIII

Family of Five

As I was slowly emerging from the depths of my grief, I felt I should see Barbara less often or not at all. I had become so dependent on our therapy sessions and this bothered me. I didn't like allowing myself dependency of any kind.

I know I should go less often or not at all.

Once again, I was beating myself up and was unable to recognize my own needs. I expressed this to Barbara in one of my visits.

I am so disappointed in myself for how I have handled the time since Mom's death—how I haven't had the inner strength I always thought I had.

Whenever I wanted to cry, but couldn't, I felt physical symptoms—fuzzy head, anxiety, racing heart. I wanted it all to stop.

Early in 2001, at the age of 37, I stopped journaling, but not before an important conversation with Barbara.

I can't seem to journal anymore though I continue to think and feel
so much. But today I asked Barbara if she thought I did everything I
could have for Mom at the end of her life. She said, "yes."

This was a significant conversation before Barbara went away for three months. Barbara's words helped ease my feelings of guilt and regret and helped me move forward.

In 2001, Jeff and I had big decisions to make. We were happy in our new home, Jeff was working for a big law firm, and I loved being a full time mom to Rebecca while also engaging in volunteer activities. We had great friends and a happy life.

Our infertility doctor wanted us to give serious thought to attempting in vitro fertilization (IVF). There was still no medical explanation for our inability to conceive and I was now in a much better place emotionally. He felt we were strong candidates for success.

Though coping with secondary infertility certainly impacted our lives, we never felt sorry for ourselves. We were ever-grateful to have our precious Rebecca. Yet, at times we felt envious of our friends who by now had two or even three children.

I was scared of IVF—I didn't want to do anything "unnatural." The thought of using hormones exacerbated my fear of getting cancer. I was already at higher risk for breast cancer. I could not put hormones in my body that could increase that risk.

I never let myself feel the emotions of secondary infertility, almost as if I hadn't learned anything from my grief journey. I focused on how we had been blessed with Rebecca and how fortunate we were compared with other loving couples who were unable to have any biological children. Any feelings of envy for friends were internalized.

We enjoyed our good life as a family of three while at the same time agonizing privately about our options for adding another child to our loving family. With each month that went by, our stress levels increased.

I had wanted to have another baby while Mom was alive and living in Rhode Island. She had missed so much of Rebecca's first year. Though she was dying at the time, I had told her that the baby would be named after her if it were a girl. I knew that made her very happy.

As we continued to consider the pros and cons of IVF, I gathered as much information as I could about the risks. I was still terrified of increasing my risk of getting cancer and suffering as Mom did.

My dear friend, Denise, was a physician and made time to gather medical research for me. I sat in my car with her at the beach as she went over the research findings. I had never been a risk-taker and this was the biggest decision I had faced. Jeff respected that this was my body and supported whatever decision I made. I was 37-years-old approaching my 38th birthday that summer of 2001.

September 11, 2001 was a beautiful day. The sun was shining and there was not a cloud in the sky. Rebecca had turned eight the previous month and was happy at school, having recently started third grade. I headed to Starbucks to meet a friend for coffee. I was looking forward to helping her plan her daughter's upcoming Cinderella-themed birthday party. While at Starbucks, a friend came in and said she had just heard on her car radio that a plane had hit the World Trade Center in New York City. At that moment in time, we thought this was nothing more than a horrible accident.

Fast forward a few hours, and Jeff and I were outside Rebecca's elementary school along with many more parents than usual. We were wondering how to tell our bright, happy eight-year-old not only that her after school playdate was cancelled, but more importantly, that the worst act of terrorism on American soil had taken place earlier that day. Four jumbo airplanes, loaded with fuel for cross-country flights, were hijacked and deliberately used as missiles, aimed at the twin towers of the World Trade Center, the Pentagon, and likely the Capitol or White House in Washington, D.C. Their intention was to kill as many Americans as possible.

This was one of those days where everyone would remember where they were when the first plane hit. Jeff and I took Rebecca home and tried to calmly explain to her what had happened while transfixed by the horror being revealed on the television. I recall the feelings of discomfort, when upon hearing about the subsequent planes that were flown into buildings, that this unequivocally was no accident.

Our country came together like never before, exhibiting patriotism and human kindness at its best. Yet, the foundation of our sense of security in our own country was crushed beyond repair. The impact was felt globally.

As life slowly returned to the new post 9/11 normal, we were left with a powerful reminder of the fragility of human life. We would have to live with uncertainty, and the knowledge that heinous acts of terrorism were no longer confined to faraway lands, but rather the unthinkable could become the next reality at any time in any place.

Personally, the events of September 11, 2001, solidified my decision to try one cycle of IVF.

> *Life is short and unpredictable and we should just go for it. Plus, not doing it doesn't guarantee any protection from cancer.*

I was risk averse and until then had been unwilling to take fertility drugs. Before the events of 9/11, Jeff and I had decided not to try IVF, but we found ourselves agonizing over the decision because we were not ready to give up our dream for another baby.

> *Contrary to how we thought we would feel we found ourselves unable to accept that this was it.*

We hoped and prayed that one cycle of IVF would not have any long term, negative consequences. After many years of unexplained secondary infertility and the recent tragic events of 9/11, we found ourselves meeting with our infertility specialist to finalize the details, timing, and consent for one cycle of IVF. There was much to endure, both physically and emotionally, but the process was underway by September 17. Now, there was no turning back.

My close friend, Michele, was a nurse. She stopped by each morning for many consecutive days to give me a hormone shot in the thigh. This was the first stage in a multi-step process. There was daily blood work and ultrasounds and eventually an egg retrieval procedure. In mid-October 2001, four healthy embryos were implanted into my uterus. From there, we entered a time of waiting, hoping, and praying.

After not one, but two pregnancy tests, my doctor confirmed on October 28, 2001, that I was pregnant. We learned this news on the 15th anniversary of Dad's death. We were cautiously optimistic, but the question remained, "how many embryos had been implanted?" Rebecca was so excited to find out she was finally going to be a big sister.

We shared our news with family and friends. Although it was so early in the pregnancy, our friends, who had been so supportive during the IVF process, were anxious to know. It was hard to keep it a secret.

The symptoms of early pregnancy set right in.

Besides fatigue and tight pants, I was faced with significant morning sickness. Not pleasant at all, but the sign of a healthy pregnancy!

We were not scheduled for our first ultrasound until about two weeks later, on November 13, 2001, at Women & Infants Hospital in Providence.

We left there in shock having learned that I was pregnant with triplets. Yes, there were three distinct sacs.

We decided to tell people that there were at least two babies. We needed time to process what we saw on the ultrasound, and I would have another ultrasound in two weeks. Our joy was now tinged with shock and nervous uncertainty.

Before the scheduled follow up ultrasound, I experienced some bleeding. Scared that I might be losing the pregnancy, I went right in for an ultrasound. I was relieved and grateful to see three flickering heartbeats. At this time, I officially was transferred from the infertility practice to the high-risk obstetrics practice at Women & Infants Hospital.

Because of intermittent bleeding, I was advised to stay off my feet and rest as much as possible. I had never been good at resting, but I would do anything to ensure a healthy pregnancy.

December brought the holiday season, the end of morning sickness, a growing belly, and a difficult situation. I was physically small and the concern was whether I would be able to successfully carry a triplet pregnancy. Even thinking about the possibility of a reduction procedure whereby the pregnancy could be reduced from a triplet to twin pregnancy was heart-wrenching for me.

My doctor, understanding our emotional roller coaster, suggested we consult with a specialist in Boston who could assist with the difficult decision we needed to make. The Boston specialist in high risk multiple pregnancies reviewed the risks of continuing a triplet pregnancy and explained the spe-cialized reduction procedure which could be performed in Boston but not Providence. The consultation was helpful but did not make this tough deci-sion any easier. I sought comfort from the minister of my church. He pro-vided spiritual support and prayed with me.

Less than a week before Christmas, we returned to the New England Medical Center. The doctor, with whom we had consulted previously, per-formed detailed ultrasound scans of the babies before sharing shocking news. One baby had not developed a brain and therefore would never be viable. The other two babies appeared healthy. Because the heart was still beating in the baby with no brain, I had a procedure without delay to stop the beating heart.

While losing the third baby certainly felt like a loss, the baby had no chance at life and now there would be more room and a better chance for a healthy twin pregnancy.

We felt tremendous relief and I was grateful for God's "divine interven-tion" in making the reduction decision for us. A triplet pregnancy was not meant to be.

Jeff had become more comfortable with Christmas and enjoyed the tradi-tions that were important to Rebecca and me. We spent Christmas Eve with good friends who were also an interfaith family. Rebecca and their three girls baked frosted sugar cookies together Christmas Eve morning and they all returned for dessert in the evening. Jeff, Rebecca, and I spent a happy Christ-mas day as a family of three, with two healthy babies growing inside me.

January 2002 was another challenging month in my pregnancy. There were several unscheduled visits to the emergency room at Women & Infants Hospital. I had multiple bouts of severe pain from fibroids. Tylenol with codeine, the strongest thing I could take, brought minimal relief. I also needed two hours of intravenous fluids at the hospital to prevent further symptoms of dehydration. At my doctor's urging, I needed to meet with a nutritionist at the hospital to ensure I was eating enough nutritious food to support the health of two growing babies and myself. Consuming enough food for a twin pregnancy was no small feat.

I had significant cravings and aversions which changed over the course of my three trimesters. The owner of our local bagel shop seemed to know whether my craving this week was egg salad or if I had moved on to corn beef. As one who ate little red meat, I was surprised to find that throughout my pregnancy I craved red meat, especially meatballs which I had never liked. One day I spontaneously went into a restaurant by myself because I absolutely had to immediately eat a hamburger, French fries with catsup, and a vanilla milkshake.

January was significant in a positive way in that fetal movement occurred at 16 weeks.

> *Rebecca put her hand on my belly and felt one of the babies move. She was so excited.*

I left the house for doctors' appointments, picking up Rebecca from school, and occasional lunch dates with friends. Jeff was supportive, working his usual long hours and taking care of laundry and grocery shopping. Eight-year-old Rebecca helped with any chores we asked of her. At home, I relaxed on the couch reading, doing the daily crossword puzzle and watching TV. The Australian Open tennis entertained me in January and the 2002 Winter Olympics in Salt Lake City did the same in February. Friends drove Rebecca to and from her activities and when she was at home, we cozily watched her favorite shows together.

February, despite the snow and cold, was a special time in my eventful and challenging pregnancy. Jeff accompanied me to my high level ultrasound.

> *We watched anxiously as the technician took lots of pictures, measurements, and went through all the body parts and organ systems of each baby.*

We told the technician that we wanted to know the sex of the babies. We were told "twin A" was a girl and "twin B" was a boy.

> *We were so excited, one of each, so perfect! The best news of all was when the doctor came in to tell us the babies looked great—exactly how they should be.*

We felt a huge sense of relief and incredible joy with this news, especially as it came after several difficult weeks filled with intermittent pain.

I asked Jeff to drive us to Barrington Beach.

With tears of joy and gratitude, I thanked God for the wonderful news we received today. I felt overwhelming gratitude and needed this time at the beach, my spiritual sanctuary.

We were excited to share our news with Rebecca after school that afternoon.

Rebecca screamed out with joy and jumped up and down. She had tears in her eyes. What a precious time for our family.

We decided that this was an appropriate time to choose names for our babies and to plan and shop for the nursery. By now I was leaving home only for doctors' appointments and we rented a wheelchair for shopping excursions. I chose stars, moons, and teddy bears as the theme for the nursery, in part because I had been wishing upon the stars for so many years. During long days on the couch, I loved perusing catalogues and the Internet for baby items.

Further ultrasounds showed that the babies were growing beautifully. My sole job was to rest and stay off my feet. Friends not only helped with chauffeuring Rebecca, but also arranged for full dinners to be delivered. I will always be grateful for the help we received. I had never been so dependent on others. This dependency was difficult to accept, but I had no choice. My friends were excited for us and happy to help.

In April, Jeff painted and prepared the nursery, Rebecca attended a "sibling class" at the hospital, and I was treated to a very special Baby Shower hosted by several dear friends and attended by a large circle of friends. I appreciated the thoughtfulness and generosity extended to me and the precious babies whose arrival we eagerly awaited.

Though my due date was in early July, I was told that if I could make it to Memorial Day, May 27, 2002, the babies should be fine. The day after Memorial Day, my water broke just after midnight. We woke Rebecca and, as planned, took her to the home of our close friends with whom we celebrated every Christmas Eve. I called my doctor who said to come right to the hospital. He said, *"It's show time."*

My pregnancy had lasted for 34 ½ weeks and it was time. I don't think my body could have carried two babies much longer. I could barely walk by this point. I was made comfortable in the labor room. The babies were both head down and fetal monitors showed that the babies were doing great. Thanks to an epidural, I was very comfortable. Jeff remained by my side, and we patiently waited for my contractions to increase in both frequency and intensity.

As the next day turned into the evening of May 29, the babies were ready to be delivered. Because of the multiple deliveries, I was wheeled into the operating room in case an emergency caesarean section was needed. The operating room was a bit like a circus. There was a neonatal intensive care team in place for each baby, an anesthesiologist, doctors, and nurses for me. After years of secondary infertility, the emotional and physical rollercoaster of IVF, and an extremely challenging pregnancy, the delivery was relatively easy! With only a few pushes, at 7:39 p.m. on May 29, 2002, Matthew Sebastian Brenner entered this world, followed 46 minutes later at 8:25 p.m. by his twin sister, Alexis Denonn Brenner.

Euphoria and relief. It was surreal

Matthew weighed 5 pounds, 3 ounces, and Alexis weighed 5 pounds, 2 ounces. They were both 18 inches long. Hospital protocol stipulated that all preemies go to the NICU after birth for observation. While I recovered, Jeff made the necessary phone calls to share our big news. On the way to my room, I was wheeled through the NICU where I was able to take pictures of my new babies. They were doing so well that within a few hours, they were taken from the NICU up to my room. They were tiny, but they had arrived and were healthy. I nursed them and tried to get some sleep.

The next day, Jeff brought Rebecca to meet her new brother and sister, and he captured this introduction on video! What a special time. We were now a family of five.

On June 1, we brought Matthew and Alexis home and a wonderful new chapter of our lives began. Family and friends were excited to meet the newest members of our family. Because they were preemies, we followed recommendations and no one but us held them for the first six weeks. We received much love and support, cards and gifts, visits and well wishes.

Jeff soon returned to work, and Rebecca finished up third grade. I happily cared for the babies. Sleep came in short spurts as I fed the babies around the clock. This was an exhausting time, but I was happy and content. Alexis and Matthew brought a deep sense of joy and happiness that I hadn't felt for years.

Rebecca adored her sister and brother who soon became known affectionately as Lexi and Matty. Rebecca was a big helper whether it was bath time or playtime.

I no longer worked part time for the hospital and I resigned from the Board of Interfaith Healthcare Ministries after a change in leadership. During my pregnancy, I had been physically unable to attend meetings so this was the right time for both resignations. I was unable to see my therapist, Barbara, during most of my pregnancy, and she moved to the west coast soon after the twins were born. Delving into my past with Barbara's skilled guidance and compassion had helped me immeasurably, but now I considered that journey completed.

I put all my time and energy into caring for the twins and Rebecca. Rebecca loved school and her activities, and the twins spent a lot of stroller time on the sidelines of Rebecca's many soccer games.

The twins reached most important milestones, like sitting up and crawling, within days of each other. They soon grew from tiny preemies into happy, healthy, average sized babies. As they got a little older, they were more fun for Rebecca and the babies loved watching her and receiving her attention. We celebrated the twins' first birthday with a smiley face themed party. I created a large poster, titled "a year of smiles" with pictures from each month of the babies' first year. We truly were celebrating a year of smiles.

By the time the infants became toddlers, we had met two other sets of twins in our town. We enjoyed playdates, story time at the library, and long stroller walks, which were my only exercise at this time. After school each day, with the twins in their car seats in our new minivan, we took Rebecca to her activities. Jeff worked long hours and weekends too, but he was always available to coach Rebecca's soccer teams. He also helped by feeding Matty his bedtime bottle while I nursed Lexi who would not take a bottle during her first year. We were a busy and happy family of five. Friends whose children were school-aged, loved any time they could see the babies.

The twins worshipped their big sister Rebecca, and she gave them her unconditional love and attention. Life was good. I felt at peace and fulfilled as a full time mother of three. I was sad that Mom never got to meet Alexis Denonn, named after her as promised, nor Matthew, whose name meant "a gift from God." But we kept Mom's memory alive as we lived life to the fullest as a family of five.

CHAPTER XIV

Asthma Brings New Challenges and a Full-Blown Eating Disorder

The twins enriched our lives beyond measure and I was completely happy in my daily life as the mother of three precious children. Starting when the twins were babies, we took our family of five on vacations during Rebecca's school breaks. We took two of everything (pack and plays, booster seats, double stroller) on our family road trips, and the twins were both flexible and adaptable with new travel routines.

With Rebecca's passion for history, our trips usually centered around visiting historic sites and Presidential Homes. We would often find a children's museum where I would entertain the twins. We also enjoyed family trips to visit relatives in Washington, DC and trips to the Lighthouse Inn on Cape Cod, the site of happy childhood memories for me.

When the twins were a little older, we loved exploring new cities from Quebec City to the north to Charleston, South Carolina to the south, and as far west as Chicago. Before each trip, I enjoyed planning our vacation details, including hotels, tourist attractions, and identifying specific places of interest for Rebecca and the twins. While traveling, I kept a travel journal and took many pictures. Upon our return home, I would make a scrapbook, including memorabilia such as every ticket stub, brochure, and restaurant business cards.

At home, I started several fun neighborhood traditions that the moms and their children looked forward to throughout the year. Events included the annual Halloween Costume Parade, Caroling, Easter Egg Hunt, Back to School Ice Cream Sundae Party, and a Last Day of School Popsicle Party. We adopted less fortunate families at Christmas time to teach our own children important lessons about helping others.

We established a neighborhood moms' group which gathered once a month to enjoy wine and conversation. We did "Secret Santa" within our group at Christmas time. We were there for each other during challenging times and shared anything that was on our minds, especially related to our children, the schools, and the town.

By the summer of 2005, the twins had recently turned three and that fall would be starting nursery school at Barrington Early Childhood Center. Rebecca was nearing her 12th birthday and would soon start seventh grade at Barrington Middle School. At that time, her passions were history and soccer, and she also enjoyed guitar and tennis lessons. A favorite place during summer was our swim and tennis club where many of our friends were also members.

That summer, at the age of 41, I started to experience random episodes of shortness of breath. I had no idea what was causing these episodes, having always been in good health. What could possibly be wrong with me? As the summer progressed and the episodes continued, I became more concerned. By late August, several scary asthma-like attacks had made breathing a struggle. Feeling devoid of energy, I was experiencing shortness of breath upon any exertion.

My focus right then, however, was on the start of the new school year. Lexi and Matty started three mornings a week at the same nursery school Rebecca had attended nine years earlier. The transition was smooth and the twins and I made many new friends. Playdates, playground time, library story time, and birthday parties made for a busy social life. Meanwhile, Rebecca was a top student and played on a travel soccer team.

My symptoms, however, could no longer be ignored, despite my preferred focus on "mom life." My doctor ordered a battery of diagnostic heart and lung tests. Terrified that something was seriously wrong, I scheduled all appointments during "school time" to avoid interfering with our busy after-noons. The tests came back negative, except for pulmonary function testing which confirmed the diagnosis of asthma.

I have to learn to manage a disease I know nothing about. I have entered a world of daily medicine, triggers, inhalers, spacers, and peak flows.

The first step was referral to a pulmonologist who could help me to iden-tify triggers and determine the medication needed for optimal asthma con-trol. My asthma doctor was well-respected and had many years of experience as a pulmonologist. He was good-natured and exuded a laid-back demeanor. He prescribed medication to take twice a day, regardless of symptoms and prescribed a rescue inhaler for when symptoms were particularly trouble-some, such as chest tightness or shortness of breath. However, he did not explain what asthma was, and he did not demonstrate how to use the inhaler. At the time, I didn't know what questions to ask.

My easygoing pulmonologist did not explain the potential gravity of asthma nor the physical and emotional impact of my chronic disease. Rather, he suggested that my asthma could ease with menopause. He also said the goal in managing my symptoms would be to lower the medication doses and perhaps stop taking them altogether.

Fortunately, my close friend Cindy was a respiratory therapist and cer-tified asthma educator. She kindly explained in detail how asthmatic lungs were different from healthy lungs and how inflammation in the airways made breathing more difficult. She patiently answered my questions and showed me how to use an inhaler and spacer to maximize the amount of medicine that goes into the lungs. Cindy's patience, support, and expertise were invaluable at a time when I was feeling overwhelmed with the diagnosis. I am forever grateful for her "Asthma 101" class which helped me to feel more capable of managing a chronic disease about which I knew little.

However, when I continued my activities, even during asthmatic flare ups, Cindy became increasingly frustrated with me for not taking my asthma seri-ously enough and for not curtailing activities in response to these flare ups.

In the first few years after my 2005 diagnosis, several serious flare ups occurred. I did not know how to stop, rest, take care of myself, or let others help. I did not want to add to Jeff's stress and I was accustomed to going non-stop and being the mom I loved to be.

Often for these flare ups, I was prescribed the oral steroid, prednisone, in addition to my regular inhalers. While this powerful medication was deemed necessary to decrease the inflammation in my lungs, the side effects were difficult to bear. Prednisone made me feel as if I had the flu. I experienced a myriad of side effects such as feeling achy, tired, and irritable. I also had no energy, no appetite, and experienced sleeplessness at night.

At times during these bad flare ups, the shortness of breath left me struggling to take a short walk or go up and down the stairs. Yet, in my mind, rest was not an option, no matter how much my asthmatic lungs needed it. I did not know how to "give in" to a disease that at times required days of rest and reduced activity.

> I lost it today emotionally when I was alone. I felt angry and frustrated and had a good cry. ASTHMA SUCKS.

I felt the need to be in control at all times, especially when caring for my children, but asthma was making me feel out of control and was preventing me from being the "on the go mom" I loved to be.

While I had "black and white" thinking, a symptom of anxiety yet to be diagnosed, asthma medications and dosages fell into a gray area of uncertainty. The gray area of asthma medications required trying different inhalers and doses to find those that best alleviated my symptoms. This trial and error with medications increased my feelings of being out of control. The way I process information, I wanted to be told why a particular medication would be better for me than another option, how the medication would impact my symptoms, what side effects to expect, and when to adjust the dosage. Instead, I was told "Try this, and we will see how it affects your symptoms, then we will figure out whether to adjust the dosage or move to another medication." This was frustrating for me.

As someone who rarely took Advil for a headache, I struggled to accept that I needed daily medications and something as strong as prednisone for flare ups. Even for a skilled physician, when to prescribe prednisone was often a judgment call. Given my acute symptoms, the prescribing of the prednisone was justified but I resisted taking it and always questioned whether there was an alternative. I had to learn how to live within the gray area of uncertainty.

I also did not use my rescue inhaler as often as required, even when it could have helped me. I considered the inhaler as necessary for emergencies only, rather than for relief of troublesome symptoms such as chest tightness. This was another gray area in which I struggled. I was unsure when to use my rescue inhaler and tested my limits by ignoring it when experiencing symptoms.

Even with my daily medication, I wanted the minimum dose possible and resisted recommendations to increase the dose due to worsening symptoms. Being in great physical shape as an athlete allowed me to be more active than others would have been able to tolerate.

I was not an easy patient. I attended all appointments, but asked many more questions than my doctor had time or desire to answer. Maybe it was the lawyer in me that questioned recommendations, but the reason was more likely due to the anxiety and loss of control that I felt in attempting to manage an illness that was more gray and uncertain, than black and white.

When my doctor did not supply the answers, I became dependent on Cindy to provide explanations and information.

My mindset throughout was more like that of a rebellious adolescent than a mature adult. Instead of taking care of myself by resting and taking the recommended medication, I challenged myself to maintain my responsibilities and activities and push my limits on the minimum possible dose of medications.

> *I don't know why I can't change my behavior and slow down when my asthma symptoms get bad. I often keep doing more almost as if to test how far I can go.*

At times, however, pushing through became impossible. I felt my body was failing me during stretches when I had no energy, experienced significant shortness of breath, and couldn't do anything other than lay on the couch. My anxiety increased when I could neither take care of my children's needs nor handle my responsibilities at home. I had to delegate some roles to Jeff who was always inundated with professional responsibilities. He never complained, but I felt guilty.

I feel so isolated and alone. Last night I cried myself to sleep which was horrible for my breathing. I am really struggling.

No one had explained the emotional impact of living with a chronic illness. These flare ups were taking a toll on my mental health.

Many years would pass before I understood that my underlying mental health issues were impeding efforts to manage my asthma in a healthier way.

Cindy, frustrated that I was not taking care of myself, urged me to see a therapist to help cope with the emotional impact of asthma as well as learn helpful skills for managing flare ups. In my mind, though, I was done with therapy. Barbara had moved to the west coast at the same time as my grief turned to joy with the birth of the twins. The thought of seeing a new therapist about my asthma was distressing. I held onto Cindy's list of suggested names and numbers for a while.

I don't know if I can make the call.

The reality was that I was extremely hard on myself. My asthma was causing severe anxiety and during especially difficult flare ups, I would become depressed or, in my words, fall into an asthma funk.

Help! I am feeling so much anxiety inside. I feel like I am spinning my wheels. Where is this all going? I just want to cry or explode. There is so much inside me and I don't know why.

A few years after my 2005 diagnosis, I finally made the call to a new therapist and after a few visits I was diagnosed with anxiety and mild depression. I learned that my anxiety and depression were not caused by asthma, but rather the anxiety and depression had pre-existed and these underlying mental health issues were negatively impacting efforts to care for myself in a sensible way.

Even with the knowledge that I suffered from anxiety, which probably originated with my parents' divorce, I did not know how to change my behavior. Cindy, who had been patient and had helped me understand my disease, became very upset at my poor handling of a particularly difficult flare up.

Cindy and I had a horrible conversation. She is upset with me for not taking asthma seriously and not putting myself first and taking care of me. I was so upset when we got off the phone. I drove to the beach either needing to scream or have a really good cry.

Cindy was one of my closest friends and had helped me so much with my asthma that I had become deeply dependent on her. She cared about me as a friend but as an expert on asthma, she could no longer stand by, watching me make decisions that put me at risk for a severe asthma attack.

Help! I don't know how to do this right. There are not many things that could be worse in my life than to have her upset with me. All I wanted was compassion and TLC.

The truth was I hated feeling weak and vulnerable. When feeling this way due to asthma symptoms I could not control, I went into a downward spiral. I wanted and needed for Jeff to think of me as strong and healthy. I didn't want to add to his stress. I had always taken care of everyone's needs, not understanding that I, too, had needs that needed tending to especially when not well. Instead of allowing myself to be cared for, I became unintentionally defiant. I did not know any better. My actions or lack thereof put a strain on my precious friendship with Cindy. I internalized the deep sadness which was the only way I knew to handle difficult emotions.

My asthma diagnosis had come in 2005 when the twins were in nursery school and Rebecca was in middle school. A few short years later when the twins were in kindergarten and Rebecca was starting high school, I began to play tennis again. Though Rebecca's passion had been soccer, she was also good at tennis and wanted to try out for the varsity team as a freshman. I had been playing some tennis socially but now also began hitting with Rebecca to help her get ready for tryouts. She was happy to make the varsity tennis team in her freshman year, in the fall of 2007.

The twins were in kindergarten that year. While they were in school, I started hitting once a week with a woman who had been a top player in Rhode Island. My consistent groundstrokes returned and I felt great! After thinking for years that my tennis was a thing of the past, I now looked forward to playing each week. Unfortunately, I also learned that exercise made my asthma symptoms worse. I struggled with when to use my inhaler, even when I knew it would help me breathe better on the tennis court.

I probably should have used my inhaler but didn't. What is wrong with me?! Why didn't I take my Xopenex when I needed it?

Rebecca's high school tennis coach was in his 80s and clearly needed help. During Rebecca's sophomore season, I became the volunteer assistant coach. I loved my new role helping the girls with strategy and how to think on the court. I added conditioning and drills to work on at practice. I supported and encouraged them during their matches.

The twins were now in school all day, in first grade. The woman I had been hitting with once a week was moving to Florida, but she introduced me to a woman she knew who had also played college tennis and was now a busy mother of three. Liz and I started playing tennis together on a regular basis. We loved our tennis time when our kids were in school and we quickly developed a close friendship.

By this time, I had switched to a new pulmonologist because my initial specialist was winding down his practice and frequently traveling out of the country. My new doctor was pleased that I was a tennis player and said I could play even with asthma symptoms. He encouraged me to use my inhaler and push myself to be able to play tennis.

There were times, however, when symptoms were such that I physically probably should not have played tennis. My new doctor didn't give clear guidelines.

It was hot and humid, but I used my inhaler and played tennis with Liz. I feel like a rebellious adolescent. Physically, I knew I shouldn't play in the high humidity but mentally I just had to. I hope I don't pay for it later.

After another flare up prevented me from playing tennis.

HELP! I need to hit a tennis ball.

Tennis was again becoming my outlet for dealing with stress and anxiety. I resumed playing competitively and this reignited my passion for the game. I became muscular and fit. Without trying, I lost weight I did not need to lose. Tennis had defined me and my life for years. Now, by resuming high level competition and coaching, it was becoming part of my identity again. I loved my new friends, the competition and the feeling of being in great shape.

All of my tennis took place when my children were in school. After school I focused on being a full time mom, driving the children to and from their activities. During my two months of coaching in the fall, the twins were cared for happily at home by a high school age babysitter. Coaching would eventually become a second career, increasing the importance of tennis in my life.

While many aspects of reigniting the tennis passion were positive, unfortunately, tennis again became my primary coping mechanism for dealing with stress, anxiety, and difficult emotions. Tennis was a healthy outlet on many levels, but not when used as an escape as in high school and college.

My new therapist, Dr. B., besides diagnosing anxiety, also discussed its origin and how to cope with it. He strongly urged me to try medication, but I resisted that kind of help. Taking daily asthma medication for a physical illness was hard enough and, in my mind, there was no way taking an anti-depressant for mental health issues could be justified. Both Cindy and Jeff emphasized the need to go beyond my difficulty coping with asthma. They wanted me to explore my past and any factors contributing to my mental health issues and inability to manage asthma flare ups with rest and self-care.

I feel like a failure that I can't handle this better. I have to be in control and have never been allowed to fail. I can't stop all the racing thoughts. So many emotions.

Meanwhile, if my brewing eating disorder had been a pot of water simmering on the back burner, it was now on the front burner coming to a rapid boil.

My journals confirm that the seeds were being planted throughout my life, and, at some point, a full-blown eating disorder (ED) would bloom. Multiple journal entries reveal that I was overly focused on food and body image. I frequently wrote about guilt experienced after eating certain foods and I commented how certain clothes made me "feel thin." At one point in young adulthood, I mentioned that if I lost five pounds, then I would be happy. In law school, I journaled that I needed to exercise before enjoying pizza with Jeff. And, after a normal pasta dinner:

> I ate too much, especially since I didn't exercise. I felt so guilty after eating it.

The connection between food and exercise was clearly ingrained long before my eating disorder took hold.

As a child, I learned from Mom that fat was bad. I did not learn intuitive eating as a child, because Mom controlled what I ate, when I ate, and how much I ate. When I got to college, the freedom with food in the "all you could eat" dining hall was wonderful. However, two months later, when the novelty had ended and I was feeling home sick, I began restricting my food intake intentionally. Perhaps I did so to feel in control or to cope with feelings of homesickness. I restricted my food intake despite several hours of tennis and running each week. I began eating the bare minimum at each meal. This was my first memory of intentionally restricting. The behavior marked the development of another ED seed, although the illness was not ready to bloom.

The development of asthma brought the water in the pot on the stove from "simmering" to a "rapid boil." For nearly 40 years I had internalized painful or difficult thoughts and feelings. From my parents' divorce at age seven, to the complicated grief from my parents' devastating cancer deaths, and everything in between, these life experiences triggered my anxiety, depression, and ultimately full-blown eating disorder. My asthma diagnosis and return to tennis along with strain in my relationships with my close friend and also with my older daughter finally broke down my walls and allowed (ED) to take over my life.

ED surfaced as a coping tool in my mid-forties in response to my inability to manage my frequent asthmatic flare ups adequately. In 2010, when I couldn't breathe well, take care of my children in the way I was accustomed, or play tennis, the eating disorder, personified as ED, came to my rescue.

My return to tennis had led to a new, fit and muscular body, and I lost weight that I did not need to lose. The positive comments received from others about my weight loss made me feel good about myself. My reignited passion for tennis and return to a high level of competition refueled my self-esteem. My return to tennis, however, also brought a return to the coping mechanism I had relied on for much of my life. The tennis court was my sanctuary, an escape from life's stressors and difficult emotions.

I played tennis today against my better judgment. But I HAD to, it's the best therapy.

When asthma flare ups took away this outlet, ED provided another way to help me feel in control. Listening to ED reduced my anxiety, numbed difficult emotions and feelings, and eased my intense fear of weight gain that developed after returning to tennis.

I have to exercise or I can't eat what I want.

Tennis made me happy, not just the act of playing, but also the friendships and my coaching job. The court, however, also provided a welcome escape from the sadness and heartbreak I felt in my relationships with Cindy and Rebecca. The emotional pain and loss were more than I could handle so ED helped me to numb those difficult feelings. Cindy and I were no longer close friends. She could no longer tolerate what she perceived as defiance in my refusal to rest and self-care during flare-ups. She did not know the reason was anxiety and an inability to recognize my own needs and make them a priority when unwell. Cindy had generously given much support as a friend, and advice based on her expertise but being incapable of accepting it, I pushed her away with my rebellious attitude and behavior.

Rebecca at this time, in the late 2000s, was in her final years of high school. We both suffered from severe anxiety. Our triggers were different and the way our anxiety manifested itself also differed. This led to frequent clashes between us and put a serious strain on our relationship. We had always been close and I feared Rebecca would think of me as I thought of my own mother. My heart felt broken and I felt sad that somehow, I had failed Rebecca as her mom by being too controlling. Internalizing the sadness and heartbreak was all I knew. ED helped when tennis couldn't. Restricting my food intake helped me to numb feelings of hurt and sadness.

Listening to ED reduced anxiety, numbed difficult emotions and eased my intense fear of gaining weight which developed after my return to tennis.

My weight loss, about 10 pounds off my small frame, was noticed by my doctors. My pulmonologist asked if I was okay and advised against losing more weight. Another health care provider recommended an eating disorder program at our local psychiatric hospital and contacted my primary care physician. My primary care physician became concerned and scheduled weight checks and "chats" every few months in addition to my annual physical.

Dr. B. continued to help me cope with anxiety and asthma. He patiently listened as I described how distraught I felt about the strain in my relationships with Cindy and Rebecca. He helped me tremendously but knew nothing about eating disorders. He suggested that I consult a dietitian about the weight loss. What could possibly be wrong? I had tennis to help me cope with the difficult topics we discussed.

I used tennis more and more as an emotional outlet, just as I had in high school and college. It reduced stress, anxiety, and made me feel thin.

I always felt a need to be in control, likely as a result of many events happening that were beyond my control. My journals revealed a cry for help as a child. I wrote prayers in my journal when gripped by anxiety due to any health or safety threat. My eating disorder in my forties helped me to control the high anxiety associated with asthma that was often out of control.

Though eating disorders appear to be about food, they are actually deep-seated mental illnesses that often co-occur with anxiety, depression, post-traumatic stress disorder, substance abuse, and other disorders.

Behaviors with food are the symptom. Maladaptive and dangerous behaviors take hold as a coping mechanism, a way of numbing difficult emotions and avoiding the pain. Food is the medicine and recovery requires confronting all that is deep inside, that the behaviors with food are trying to suppress. Eating disorders are complex illnesses requiring an interdisciplinary team that includes, a therapist, a dietitian, a primary care doctor, and often a psychiatrist. Eating disorders are consuming illnesses and recovery is a difficult journey, often with many twists and turns along the way.

You can't tell by looking at someone if they have an eating disorder. I knew that I had lost weight and was restricting when I couldn't play tennis. I liked my muscular and fit body. But I was not capable of seeing myself as thin as others saw me. I saw myself through ED's eyes. Enough was never enough for ED, and ED would make sure I stayed thin.

An intense fear of gaining weight was also fueled by worry about menopause weight gain. Several women who were older than me had gained weight despite "eating well" and exercising. My primary care doctor, who was otherwise an outstanding physician, said during a weight check visit, "Don't worry, you'll have no trouble gaining weight when you hit menopause." I heard that through ED's ears, ED would make sure that didn't happen to me.

Meanwhile, Jeff had observed the worsening of many of my behaviors. He knew I was way too preoccupied with food and that I needed exercise to feel at peace. He saw evidence of my negative body image. For example, I would often change my outfits multiple times until I found one that made me "feel thin."

Dr. B. continued to suggest that I consult with a dietitian. A neighbor had been seeing one in our town for weight management so I asked for her contact information. At least a year would pass before I made that call, a call that would change my life. Jeff and I both had much to learn. The eating disorder's grip was firmly in place, and releasing ED's control over me would be exceedingly difficult.

What was my life like when I was in the throes of my eating disorder, when my brain was consumed by thoughts about food and exercise?

—

CHAPTER XV

Life With ED

Living with an eating disorder (ED) was exhausting and consuming. ED controlled me with strict rules about food and exercise. Listening to ED helped me to feel in control and maintain my thin, muscular, and fit body. But living with ED's strict rules was impairing my life and, without timely professional intervention, would have endangered my health.

ED's rules made me feel in control, but I was not truly living. I could not be fully present when many thoughts were focused on exercise and food. Some foods, such as sweets, were forbidden except for a few exceptions: an occasional frozen yogurt, a bite or two of birthday cake, and one home-baked sugar cookie on Christmas Eve.

On weekend nights, Jeff and I loved going out to dinner with friends at a nice restaurant. ED had me jump through hoops, so to speak, in order to enjoy a social evening. I absolutely had to exercise, preferably vigorous tennis, and restrict my food intake during the day. It was as if I had to earn a good dinner out with friends. The exercise and food restriction during the day were essential for me to feel at peace that evening when eating bread, perhaps a salad with salmon or shrimp, a half of a glass of prosecco, and possibly a few bites of a shared dessert. If going out to dinner after several consecutive days of vigorous tennis, ED allowed me to splurge and order my favorite meal—eggplant parmesan. I always stopped before I was full, even when I easily could have eaten more. Another favorite food after vigorous tennis was sweet potato fries but always with salad, and shrimp or salmon.

A treat on summer nights out was a frozen strawberry daiquiri. Since I rarely drink, I would consume only maybe half of this sweet, filling drink. And when ED did allow this drink, there would definitely be no dessert of any kind.

Casual weekday lunches out with friends involved ED always coming along, and reassuring me that I was not like my friends who talked about "having to be good" with food or how they had gained five pounds over the holidays. ED made sure I always felt in control. However, ED, not me, was the one in control.

Breakfast at home was never an issue. I would awaken feeling hungry each morning and eat a good size bowl of cereal, a mix of several favorite kinds, a small glass of orange juice, and a big mug of coffee with whole milk. This was the only meal I could eat with no ED thoughts attached, because this has been my morning routine for as long as I can remember. When we travelled, however, hotel breakfasts presented a challenge. While my family enjoyed pancakes, waffles, or French toast, or a made-to-order omelet, ED insisted I have my usual cold cereal with skim milk. Because hotel bowls were smaller than our cereal bowls at home, ED allowed me to supplement the cereal with a toasted English muffin or a small muffin.

Hotels almost always have fitness centers. ED made sure I completed a 30-minute elliptical workout after breakfast even if we were going to walk miles and miles that day, exploring whatever city we were visiting.

At resort hotels, ED allowed me to skip the fitness center if playing tennis that day. Long beach walks added more exercise, but were also my favorite activity by the ocean. Even at a beautiful oceanfront resort on vacation, I wouldn't feel at peace or relaxed until my exercise was checked off my morning to-do list.

Lunch on vacation was always a salad rather than the sandwich and chips or burger and fries enjoyed by others in my family. On vacation, my children felt strongly that ice cream should be a part of every day. We would visit the best local ice cream shop after an afternoon on the beach or at the pool. ED limited my indulgence to a kiddie size scoop, and usually made me choose the low-fat frozen yogurt option rather than my favorite ice cream flavor, mint chocolate chip.

Eating three restaurant meals a day on vacation was anxiety-provoking. When I ordered my second salad of the day for dinner, my family became the food police, saying, "You ate a salad for lunch." I would add shrimp or salmon for protein and if I had exercised, perhaps sweet potato fries, a favorite of mine. Only on those rare days without ice cream, would I consider ordering a frozen drink to enjoy with dinner.

At home, lunch was often a challenge. I have never been a big sandwich eater. Even as a young girl, Mom would pack peanut butter on saltine crackers rather than a sandwich in my Snoopy lunch box. I tended to graze, substituting a series of snacks, rather than sitting down to eat a turkey sandwich for lunch. I felt more comfortable with options such as a protein bar and fruit. Sometimes when I was extra hungry after tennis, I would eat a muffin or bagel. At dinner, Jeff noticed I would move my food around my plate to make it look like I was eating more than I actually did.

I never intentionally skipped meals, but I was not a snacker and especially did not eat anything at night after dinner. Sometimes, however, what one might consider a snack was a meal for me. The bottom line was that I was depriving my body of the fuel it needed.

I loved coming off the tennis court after a strenuous match or practice. Tennis reduced my anxiety and helped me to feel at peace. Tennis was also my ticket to eating more food and restricting less. Upon my return to tennis in my mid-40s, I developed an intense fear of gaining weight and ED would make sure that didn't happen. Both tennis and my thin, muscular, and fit body made me feel good about myself.

I kept my eating disorder a secret from almost everyone in my life. When coaching, I would tell the girls how to fuel their bodies to practice and compete at their best, yet I wasn't properly fueling my own several hours of tennis each week.

I felt deep shame being an adult with an eating disorder. Anyone not familiar with this illness would assume that if I would "just eat", the eating disorder would somehow simply disappear. If only it were that easy. One friend said, "Don't let that happen," as if the eating disorder was a choice. Another friend expressed words of support when I finally got the courage to tell her my secret, but she never mentioned it again. I don't blame my friends. The harsh reality is that there is little to no understanding about eating disorders. The misconceptions about this complex psychiatric illness run rampant and are unfortunately perpetuated in the media. Furthermore, eating disorders do not discriminate. These life-threatening illnesses affect men and women, boys and girls, and people of all ages, shapes and sizes.

In November 2011, when Rebecca was in her first semester at Mount Holyoke College and the twins were in fourth grade, I saw a dietitian for the first time. Grace's office was in her home, less than 10 minutes from my house. At my first appointment I was diagnosed with anorexia. I was shocked by this diagnosis, thinking that to have anorexia one had to be emaciated as a result of self-starvation. I was aware that I was thin and had lost weight but I was hardly emaciated and did not skip meals. I was simply restricting my intake, avoiding sweets and other high calorie foods and burning hundreds of calories on the tennis court each week. Jeff, too, was puzzled by the diagnosis. His perception of someone with anorexia was an emaciated teenage girl.

I was a busy mother of three and a high school tennis coach. I did not fit either of our preconceived stereotypes. I had little to no understanding of this battle that was consuming me every day. But now I was under the care of Grace, a registered dietitian with expertise in the treatment of eating disorders.

On appointment days, I would wait in my car in front of Grace's house until I saw the previous client walk out the door and get into their car. I would then follow the walkway to the front door. On arrival, Grace would swing open the front door, greet me warmly upon entering, and follow me into her office immediately to the right. Grace was warm and kind and always professionally and stylishly dressed. She had a way about her that made me feel comfortable. She sat in her desk chair turned toward a round glass table. I sat in a chair across the table from her.

Grace reassured me that my eating disorder was not my fault and not my choice, but rather a brain-based disorder. She told me:

> This illness is bigger than you and you cannot do it alone. It is not your fault. You didn't ask for this, you don't want it and getting support is not a sign of weakness.

Grace recommended books and articles to help me understand my illness. My favorites were Jenni Schaefer's *Life Without Ed* and *Goodbye Ed, Hello Me.* Often, during my appointments, Grace would take one of these books off her shelf, turn to a page tagged with a yellow sticky note, and use the passage to help reinforce something we were talking about.

Grace created meal plans for me to follow. She did so in a way that was not overwhelming, gradually adding more nutrition to restore my weight. Some of the new foods I added early on were chocolate milk and almonds. I was supposed to eat three meals and two snacks every day. Nowadays, dietitians use apps with their clients to communicate between appointments. Logging meals keeps the client accountable. Grace had me start emailing her every night with details of what I had consumed that day. She responded to every email with comments about my nutrition and also encouraging and inspiring words.

> *Nice job with the whole sandwich and milk today. You CAN do this. Only focus on one meal at a time. "Do the next right thing."*

In addition to recounting what I ate in my emails, I would sometimes express how I was feeling.

> *ED absolutely exhausts me every single day. When I do the next right thing, ED's voice is louder and I feel worse.*

Grace would respond in her reassuring way.

> *ED makes you feel shame, obsess about food, restrict and use exercise to justify eating. You are starting to engage in recovery. It is hard but it is worth it. I know you are trying really hard.*

This daily email exchange was a source of tremendous support and this connection helped me especially during the many weeks of the year when Grace travelled. I became dependent on the email support. I saved many of her inspiring words and added them to my quote book.

Trust your body. It will take good care of you. You are strong and
determined. Believe in yourself. You can do this.

Grace reassured me that our daily emails were not a burden. She lik-
ened this daily support to that offered in a residential program. I didn't like
being dependent, but this support was invaluable to my recovery. I would
have benefited greatly from a residential program where I could have focused
exclusively on recovery, but I was not willing to disrupt my family life, leave
my children or add to Jeff's stress.

I looked forward to my appointments with Grace. Her caring words
made me feel comfortable enough to eventually open up and gradually let
my guard down. Our conversations went beyond nutrition and meal plans.
Though we did need to spend significant time talking about what I could
add to my meal plan to help my recovery, we began to talk about my life and
about my eating disorder, both what contributed to it and what continued to
trigger me.

We have one life on this earth, let's make the most of it. Keep living the
life you want to live. It's a journey and you are on a good path.

Grace helped me learn to eat sweets again in her office. I would bring a
new challenge food to her office for us to share. I remember bringing cup-
cakes or different kinds of cookies. She would cut the treat in half for us to
share. She supported me as I took that first bite.

Don't be afraid. Trust the process.

Eventually, if my appointment were scheduled for lunch time, I would
bring a sandwich, my chocolate milk, and a dessert for us to share. She would
have her sandwich ready on a plate and we would eat our lunches together
while we talked.

One day, Grace gave me a Dove dark chocolate to try. I hadn't eaten a
single piece of candy for as long as I could remember. The chocolate was
wrapped in red foil and on the inside of the wrapper was always a quote.
Grace said she had a chocolate drawer in her kitchen. I started keeping a bowl

of Dove dark chocolates in my kitchen and I still eat one almost every day. I think of Grace and our years together when I have one and I have saved some of the sayings in my quote book.

Be happy. Be you.

After several months of working with Grace, and only minimal progress, she convinced me that I needed a therapist who specialized in eating disorders. Dr. B had helped to reduce anxiety following my asthma diagnosis and I felt comfortable talking to him about some of my challenges. Unfortunately, he knew little about eating disorders.

Grace contacted a well-regarded therapist in Providence on my behalf. This therapist specialized in eating disorders and I started weekly sessions with her in the summer of 2012, less than a year after my first appointment with Grace. Outpatient treatment for an eating disorder requires a well-trained team. A therapist with expertise in this field was necessary to help me identify the root of my eating disorder and identify triggers. Just as I was starting to feel comfortable with this new therapist, however, she left for a full-time position in Boston. Before departing, she arranged an appointment with a highly sought eating disorder therapist whose office was on the first floor of the same building in Providence. This next therapist, Emily, was not taking new patients, but she provided a slot for me as a favor for her colleague. I had my first appointment with Emily in March of 2013.

Beginning to work with another therapist was difficult, but Emily was the therapist I needed when starting the hard work of recovery. Besides identifying what was at the root of my eating disorder, I needed to explore and process the emotions that were being numbed by the eating disorder. This process had added complexity due to about 40 years of internalizing difficult emotions during challenging times in my life.

Emily was not only one of the smartest people I had met, but also a highly skilled, experienced, and insightful therapist. She was caring, consistent, and fully present in our 45 minute sessions. With Emily, I had a safe space where I could talk about the complicated relationships with my parents and discuss how difficult experiences had shaped me. She helped me to understand how my eating disorder had developed as a way to cope with the unspoken feelings and suppressed emotions. Emily reminded me recently that I often slammed the door as I exited her office. I craved care, but did not know how to accept it. I always felt the short sessions were never enough time to go into depth on any of the important topics we needed to discuss. Many weeks I would walk out of her office wondering how I was going to survive to the following week's appointment, having touched on difficult emotions and challenges only briefly. I imagined that if my emotions were water being held back by a dam, the water would begin to seep out during my session, but when I left there, I felt like I had to hold on with all my might to prevent the entire dam from breaking.

My sessions with Grace had been for 90 minutes, twice as long and therefore more time to get into the heart of whatever we were discussing. The conversations with Grace soon went well beyond food, nutrition, and meal plans. Slowly but surely, Grace learned about my life story and many of the challenges I had faced. She was an athlete herself and understood why tennis was important to me. She wanted me to bring the qualities that made me an outstanding competitor to the hard work of recovery. Determination, motivation, and self-belief were ingrained in me as a competitive tennis player. Recovery from my eating disorder would require those qualities and more.

> *Stay strong, stay determined, 3 real meals, 2 good snacks, and dessert! You can do this; I know you can! Just like tennis, one point at a time. Do not give up.*

Playing several hours of tennis each week meant I needed to consume more food for my recovery. A particularly difficult challenge was the need to continually fuel my body sufficiently, even on days with no exercise. Restricting and no exercise had gone hand in hand, but I had to learn that on days with no exercise, my organs still needed sufficient nutrition to function properly. While tennis improved my appetite, I had to learn to eat even when not hungry. Grace warned that if I only ate to my appetite, I would lose weight. Food was my medicine every single day.

There are no days off in recovery. The only time I felt truly supported was during my time each week with Emily and Grace. Between appointments, I had to work on recovery every day within the context of my daily life. I was secretive about my struggle while going about life as a mom, wife, high school tennis coach, bereavement group facilitator, and competitive tennis player.

Grace kept me accountable. She also gave encouragement and support every step of the way. She believed in me even when I had trouble believing in myself. The level of care and support from her was something I had felt only at one other time, and that was the care and support Steve and Patti gave me around the time of my father's death.

I will never give up on you! It's just a matter of time before you decide to do whatever it takes to take back control of your life.

Grace impressed on me that it was not enough to want recovery, but that I had to be willing to do whatever it would take. I had so much respect for Grace that when she strongly urged me to try medication, I was willing to consider it. She assured me that even a small dose of an SSRI anti-depressant could help reduce anxiety which would hopefully help quiet the ED thoughts and make it easier to eat. It wouldn't be easy, and it was no "magic pill," but Grace felt strongly that it could help my recovery and I trusted her. Eventually with the expertise of a psychiatrist, we found the dose that helped to reduce my anxiety, fortunately without any troubling side effects. A few people in my life confided in me that they were on the same medication, so I felt less shame.

Recovery required a willingness to do the hard work—eating more than I was comfortable eating, eating when I was not hungry, eating according to my meal plan on no exercise days, accepting my newly weight restored body, tolerating the discomfort of feeling full, and eventually parting with my "skinny clothes." I worked on recovery day after day, week after week, month after month, year after year. Grace always said that recovery without a formal treatment program was almost impossible. With her belief in me, care, and support, I wanted to be a success story. I wanted her to see me as recovered.

What a journey. You are reaching another level! Emotions will not drag you down. Feel them and be free. The best movies are the ones about people who overcome their challenges—they are heroes. You

are too! Stay strong, stay determined. Tell your story. It is one of vic-
tory—not defeat!

Grace helped me get through tough times when I was unable to exercise due to a significant tennis injury, asthma flare ups, and recovery from surgery. Following my meal plan was harder when exercise was taken out of the equation.

Stay focused—one day at a time. To break free, you must disobey ED.
I believe in Betsy—you are strong!

Before taking a vacation, Grace would help me talk through the plan for eating many restaurant meals. She encouraged me to be a "fearless eater."

Break any and all remaining ED rules. Make it an ED free vacation.
Challenge yourself and push your limits!

Whenever I was able to disobey ED and enjoy a mint chocolate chip ice cream cone on vacation, Jeff would take a picture of me with the ice cream and I would include the photo with my evening email. The positive reinforcement from Grace always made me feel good and helped with my recovery.

I wouldn't be where I am today without Emily. With her astute skills as a therapist and her calm and caring disposition, I was able to get in touch with the emotions which ED had numbed for me for so long. At times, Emily understood me better than I understood myself. Grace had taught me that I had needs of my own, and Emily took this further, helping me to identify what those needs were and figure out how to meet them. We talked a lot about my complicated relationship with Mom and how that was strongly associated with the development of my eating disorder.

Emily correctly characterized my relationship with Mom as one where my role was always to meet Mom's needs. I wasn't allowed to have needs of my own. I did not learn to tolerate any negative affect and became an expert at internalizing emotions. This was a form of self-protection. It took many months, even a few years, before Emily's skilled approach began to penetrate the wall, I had built around me. Emily was the key to my getting in touch with layers of suppressed emotions. It was often after I walked out her door at the end of the session that I began to feel the feelings. This was a difficult piece of recovery but necessary. I cried at times with Emily but most of the tears flowed after I left. I felt alone with the emotions, often needing time before going on with my day. I had always feared that if I started to cry, I wouldn't be able to stop. I was now learning how to feel the feelings, essential for my recovery.

Emily used many metaphors which always seemed to illustrate well whatever we were discussing. One metaphor in particular I still associate with understanding what recovery is about. While Grace always talked about a finish line for my recovery journey, Emily viewed recovery in different terms. Emily used a sailing metaphor to explain that recovery was about learning healthy coping skills for life's stressors and challenges. A sailor must become more and more skilled to be able to adjust the sails when battling the stormy seas. A quote by Louisa May Alcott, American novelist best known as the author of *Little Women* in 1868, aligns well with recovery.

I'm not afraid of storms, for I am learning how to sail my ship.

While many people fully recover from eating disorders and never hear from ED again, for others this is not an absolute. Recovery isn't necessarily about a final destination, but it is about learning a healthy way of coping with life, including challenges and difficult emotions. Just as a sailor needs to develop skills to handle stormy seas, in recovery I needed to learn how to cope with anxiety, sadness, and stress without restricting food or over exercising.

One key to my recovery was connection and support. At times the support came only from Emily and Grace. Eventually I was more open and honest with two close friends and they were able to help me by listening and encouraging me. Vulnerability, which I had always equated with weakness, was also essential for recovery.

Vulnerability opened the door to recovery by giving me the courage to be my authentic self. I learned in recovery that I didn't have to always be positive and unemotional. I had to learn that I had no reason to feel guilty for having negative emotions. I could appreciate the many blessings in my life and also feel sad or upset. A quote from Lori Deschenes, author and founder of TinyBuddha.com, profoundly depicts the mindset that was necessary for my recovery:

> *You don't have to be positive all the time. It's perfectly okay to feel sad, angry, annoyed, frustrated, scared, or anxious. Having feelings doesn't make you a 'negative person.' It makes you human.*

Healthy relationships replace eating disorders and connections with friends, with whom I could be my authentic self, strengthened my recovery. Such relationships also enabled me to find my voice and use it.

As a child, I felt I had to be perfect to earn Mom's love and approval. I had to meet her needs. In recovery I learned that I have a voice. I need to use it to ask for what I need and express what I am feeling. My eating disorder for many years did not allow me to be fully human. I had to be perfect and always in control. I first learned to let my guard down with Grace and with Emily. Their professional expertise and compassionate guidance and support eventually broke through my defenses.

In recovery I have learned that I can be human, imperfect, and feel all kinds of emotions. It's okay to have needs, and important to meet them. Self-care, which was not in my vocabulary, became of utmost importance. Self-care is not selfish. Self-care is about loving myself, meeting my needs, nourishing my body with food and nurturing my mind and spirit. In my late 50s, I continue to create my authentic self and learn who I am without my eating disorder. My sad inner child had been craving unconditional love for years, and it is up to me to give myself that love and heal the sad inner child.

Jeff's love has sustained me throughout my journey. He wants nothing more than for me to happy, healthy, and at peace. But even with my beloved husband's devotion, I felt shame as a result of my eating disorder. It was easier not to talk about it, and instead focus on enjoying our wonderful family life.

Six years after my eating disorder diagnosis, the biggest physical challenge of my life would test the strength of my recovery and herald an important chapter in my recovery story.

CHAPTER XVI

———

Gratitude

My eating disorder had been diagnosed in 2011 and I had been working hard on recovery with my outpatient team. In December 2016, five years into my recovery journey, the strength of recovery was tested by the most difficult physical experience of my life.

My doctor ordered pelvic ultrasounds every two years to follow multiple fibroids, originally discovered during pregnancy ultrasounds. They had caused severe pain during my pregnancy with the twins but fortunately had not caused further problems. My doctor was thorough in her testing, which I appreciated.

On December 8, 2016, I learned that my routine pelvic ultrasound showed a 5 cm complex cyst on my left ovary. My doctor attempted to ease my immediate fear and anxiety by reassuring me that these cysts often go away on their own and are usually related to the menstrual cycle. She said it was a good sign that I had very regular periods. She ordered a repeat ultrasound in four to six weeks to see if the cyst disappeared.

The Christmas holiday season was a wonderful distraction but when the calendar flipped to January 2017, my anxiety level began to rise. On Monday, January 16, 2017, I returned to Rhode Island Medical Imaging for my repeat ultrasound. The technician shared with me that the cyst was still there and that it had increased in size. Only Jeff's hugs could make me feel better as my anxiety made me fear the worst.

My doctor called the next day with the report from the ultrasound. Her tone was more serious than the December call and I pulled into a parking lot for the ensuing conversation. She said that the cyst was now 6.5 cm and that there were more solid components than before. She calmly, but matter of fact, in her serious tone said that because of its size, the cyst would need to be surgically removed. Pathology following surgery would be the only way to confirm what it was with certainty. She said not to be alarmed, but that she was referring me to a gynecological oncologist. Two doctor friends of mine confirmed that Dr. Bandera was the best in the state. That was reassuring but the two weeks waiting for my appointment were extremely difficult.

I spent way too much time on the Internet looking up different kinds of ovarian masses. This research only made my anxiety increase to almost unmanageable levels. I needed Ativan to sleep at night. I was worried, scared, and feared the worst. I tried to reassure myself that most of these ovarian masses were benign but the reality was that it also could be cancer.

Jeff gave me tremendous support and love and I felt cared for by close friends, some of whom were praying for me and others who were checking in with frequent calls and texts. I felt supported during this difficult time of uncertainty.

On February 1, 2017, Jeff accompanied me to my first appointment with Dr. Bandera. Her office was at Women's Medicine Collaborative, the same place I now went for asthma care. I felt comforted to see Cindy when we arrived and she gave me a big hug. Check in was adjacent to where I reported for pulmonology appointments. The sign on the desk read GYN-ONC and the receptionist answered the phone "Cancer Care Services." She was especially warm and friendly upon check in.

A nurse took a full history and then we waited for what seemed like forever for Dr. Bandera to come into the exam room. I hung on every word she said and had a glimmer of hope when she said that her gut feeling was that it probably was not cancer, but only surgery could confirm. After her exam, she said I had two tasks: blood work and a CT scan. I would then return a week later to discuss the results and plan for the surgery.

Tennis was the only outlet for this level of stress and anxiety though nothing could sufficiently distract me. I wanted to complete the two tasks as soon as possible. I was able to get blood drawn at the lab that afternoon and schedule the CT scan for the very next day.

I had planned on going to the CT scan by myself, but my friend Zoë insisted that I not go alone. Zoë accompanied me to the imaging center at the hospital. I was grateful for her support. The contrast dye used for the test made me feel "yucky" so I was relieved not to have to drive myself home. Zoë kindly took me back to her house. She made a cup of tea and we sat by the fire. I was not yet ready to go home where I had to act as if everything was normal. I didn't plan to tell the twins anything until I knew exactly what was happening. Sitting with Zoë by the fire was comforting. The tender loving care (TLC) she gave me that afternoon meant so much to me.

The days waiting for the CT scan results were extremely difficult. My anxiety was unbearable. I was in the middle of an important interclub tennis match when I noticed on my iPhone that I had a "new test result" in my patient portal. As soon as the match ended, I went outside to check the results.

A tremendous feeling of relief and gratitude came over me as I read the test results on my iPhone in the cold February air. The results disclosed that the ovarian mass was indeed there, but everything else was normal, including the lymph nodes. I showed the results to a doctor friend at the tennis club for her medical interpretation. She confirmed the good news. Now, the worst case scenario was that if cells in the mass were malignant, they were completely contained, and could be removed. Everything else was clear, meaning that surrounding organs looked normal and there was no spread whatsoever. My blood work also came back normal which was more positive and reassuring news.

My follow up appointment with Dr. Bandera was on February 8. She shared with us the good news that what we were looking at was more than likely a benign tumor. Still, it would have to be removed. Dr. Bandera had a wonderful way about her, very professional yet reassuring. I knew I would be in good hands. She discussed with us details about the planned surgery. Because large fibroids filled my uterus, she would not be able to perform the procedure laparoscopically as many hysterectomies are currently performed.

Instead of a small incision and shorter recovery, I would need a total abdominal hysterectomy with a vertical abdominal incision and a three to five day hospital stay. The plan was to remove my uterus, both ovaries, my cervix and fallopian tubes. Dr. Bandera patiently answered all of our questions and said the scheduler would be in touch with us and to expect a surgery date in about two to three weeks.

That afternoon I had an appointment with Grace. While there, I received a call from the surgery scheduler saying there was an opening on Monday, February 13, only five days away. I was glad I was with Grace with whom I felt comfortable when the reality that I would be undergoing major surgery became real. She supported me by helping me to be as strong as possible before undergoing surgery. My eating disorder did not interfere in any way. The stronger I was, the better my body would tolerate major surgery.

The weekend before my surgery was busy preparing for my hospital stay. I packed my bag, went over schedules with Jeff, gave him a list of phone numbers, and insisted that we have a conversation, a most difficult one, about my wishes should something happen to me. The twins were now freshmen in high school and I had explained to them what a hysterectomy was and answered their questions about the week ahead.

The day before my surgery, Liz and I played tennis. This would be my last tennis for at least two months and Liz understood my need to play. Later in the day, I was more worried about the snow predicted for the morning when we would be going to the hospital, than the surgery itself. Thanks to Ativan, I was able to get some sleep. I sincerely appreciated the calls, texts, and emails wishing me well for my surgery.

On Monday, February 13, I was relieved that the predicted storm never materialized. I gave the twins extra big hugs before they left for school. They would be spending the afternoon and evening at the home of a close friend until Jeff could return home from the hospital.

When Jeff and I arrived at the hospital admitting office, I was no longer anxious. It was time to have the surgery and get it over with. Everyone in the pre-op area was very nice. They reviewed the necessary information and answered my questions. I had expressed concern about my asthma and general anesthesia but the anesthesiologist kindly assured me I would get an asthma treatment in the operating room. Dr. Bandera stopped by and once again I felt I would be in excellent hands. The last thing I remember was a nurse coming in to put something in my intravenous line.

After I was wheeled to the operating room, Jeff headed to the cafeteria and then the surgical waiting area. He was anxious during the three-hour surgery awaiting news from the doctor. He found it hard to read or focus. He paced in and around the waiting area, made some work calls, spoke with concerned family members, and checked emails. Finally, Dr. Bandera emerged to share the news with Jeff that the surgery went well, there were no complications, and the best news of all, there were no signs of cancer anywhere.

I remember waking up very groggy in the recovery room and asking a nurse how the surgery went. She said "fine" which didn't exactly give me much information. They wouldn't let Jeff in the recovery room, so he used the time to call family and close friends who were anxiously waiting to hear how the surgery went and how I was doing.

I remember the long, bumpy ride through the hospital corridors with Jeff by my side. There were tunnels, elevators, and lots of bumps before I was safely transferred to my hospital bed. I was in a private room in a section of the hospital recently renovated for Women's Medicine Collaborative's patients. It was late-afternoon by the time I finally made it to my room. I felt crampy and uncomfortable and slept in short spurts. Every time I opened my eyes, Jeff was there. Jeff relayed to me his conversations with family and friends. I remember wanting to talk to him but I was having a hard time keeping my eyes open.

Dr. Bandera came to check on me and my six-inch vertical incision on my abdomen. She told me what she had told Jeff—that the surgery went well and there was no cancer. Though groggy and uncomfortable, I felt euphoria, gratitude, and relief. The surgery was over, I was alive, and I had received good news.

Jeff stayed as long as he could into the early evening. As much as I would have loved for him to be there with me, I wanted him to be able to attend our daughter Lexi's play at Barrington High School. He sped to the school and stood in the back of the auditorium for a standing-room only one-night performance. He arrived there just before Lexi's major scene. On the subsequent nights while I was in the hospital, Jeff was home with the twins to keep their lives as normal as possible.

During my first night in the hospital, a very kind CNA made me get out of bed for a short walk, IV pole and all. This task seemed impossible at first, but with her help and support, I did it slowly but surely. She brought me a purple popsicle, the only food that seemed appealing, and was my sole nutrition for the entire day. I had an IV pump for narcotic pain meds. I could push the button every eight minutes as needed. I needed it! That night, I desperately wanted to sleep but the hospital was not a place for restful sleep. The nurses woke me up constantly to check my vitals, take blood, and give me meds. I was extremely uncomfortable, even with narcotics and had a rough night with very little sleep.

The next morning, Jeff arrived after driving the twins to school. He stayed with me for hours and was totally present with me and for me. His biggest challenge was to find food that I would eat. I had no appetite and the hospital food was most unappealing. Jeff eventually got me a blueberry muffin and soft pretzel which I was able to eat.

Dr. Bandera came by each morning on her rounds, along with medical students and residents. She checked my incision and said it looked good. Jeff was with me each day and went home each afternoon to the twins. While I felt alone not having Jeff with me in the evenings, I had peace of mind knowing he was with the twins and taking care of their needs. The evenings and overnights were particularly difficult. I couldn't focus enough to read or watch television. I experienced continuous pain even with the IV pump and was exhausted from lack of sleep. I tried to rest and overall remained in good spirits, feeling grateful that I was healthy and the worst was behind me.

During the day I wasn't feeling ready for lengthy phone conversations but I welcomed visits from several close friends. Jeff and friends accompanied me on walks down the hallway. I received beautiful flowers and cards and kept in touch by text with family and friends.

Two days after my surgery, Jeff brought the twins to the hospital. They missed me at home and needed to see me. I was so happy to see them. They had never visited anyone in the hospital before. While difficult to see me in that setting, they were reassured to see that I was okay.

During my four-day hospital stay, Jeff's care and support comforted me daily. I had never felt his love and presence as profoundly as I did during my hospital stay. On Thursday, February 16, Dr. Bandera came to see me during her daily rounds and gave us the news that I could be discharged that afternoon, one day ahead of schedule. Jeff was thrilled, because he wanted to care for me in the peacefulness of our own home. My first reaction was feeling overwhelmed by the thought of getting up and dressed and the process of going home. With Jeff's help and encouragement, I made it! I felt every little bump, and held a pillow over my belly as I was advised to do during the 20-minute ride home.

I remained quite uncomfortable and on narcotic pain medication in pill form. The process of going home was exhausting, but I felt so good to be on my comfy couch and I was able to eat my first meal, scrambled eggs and rye bread toast. My appetite had not yet returned and I had struggled while in the hospital to get any real nutrition into me. I had texted Grace during my hospital stay about my lack of appetite and inability to eat hospital food. I was worried that the hard work of recovery would be lost. She reassured me that I would be okay and she would be there to support and help me.

Once settled, I felt happy to be home. My only responsibility was to rest and let my body heal. I experienced pain and discomfort requiring meds around the clock. I took little walks in my house as walking was encouraged. Friends stopped by with lots of food. Jeff and the twins were well fed but, unfortunately, I didn't have the appetite to enjoy the great dinners. Jeff was back on his laptop and phone working at the dining room table. He chauffeured the twins and took care of me and household responsibilities. Friends came by frequently and sat with me. I was surrounded with cards, gifts, and flowers, but more importantly my heart was filled with an outpouring of care, love, and support in a way I had never experienced before.

I had no choice but to rest. That first night home, as I looked up to the top of the staircase, I felt as if I had to climb a mountain to sleep in my own bed. I did it slowly and had to rest at the top of the stairs before walking down the short hallway to my bedroom. Had I not been in such great physical shape before my surgery, I likely would have had a longer and more difficult time recovering.

For many days, Jeff brought me my breakfast in bed. I would need to rest after every single activity, brushing my teeth, getting dressed, and the biggest one—taking a shower. The effort took so much out of me. I would make it downstairs to the couch by mid-morning and stay there until bedtime. I rested and took slow, short walks around my house. I neither read books nor watched movies. I watched the tennis channel, *"Friends"* reruns with the twins, and played "Words With Friends" on my iPad.

Jeff was amazing, taking care of everything with no complaints. I welcomed visits from friends, treasuring their presence, friendship, love, and support.

With prayers, gifts, flowers, food, visits, texts, and calls, I never felt alone. For the many weeks of recovery, I had to care for my body so that it could heal from major surgery. I had to nurture it with rest and nourish it with food. I took care of my body's needs surrounded by tremendous love and support.

Exactly one week after my surgery, my dear friend Patti left her sunny, warm Florida paradise to help take care of me and my family so that Jeff could return to his office.

Patti motivated me to take my first outside walk. The first one was just in front of the house, but within a few days, Patti had me walking around the block with her by my side. She made sure I ate my first "real food" since my appetite had been almost non-existent. Her encouragement succeeded in getting me to eat. Patti stayed a week with us. In addition to caring for me, she did the grocery shopping, planned and cooked meals, and drove the twins to their activities. She was simply amazing, especially given my significant limitations. My heartfelt gratitude to Patti cannot be put into words.

I left the house for the first time for a doctor's appointment with Dr. Bandera in early March. The pathology report confirmed a benign ovarian tumor. Had my primary care physician not ordered the initial ultrasound, the tumor was the type that would have grown and eventually burst. Thankfully, it had been discovered and removed in a planned fashion, not in an emergency.

Grace came over for a "house call" in early-march and brought lunch and her scale. My weight had unfortunately plummeted as a result of my lack of an appetite, but with her care, support, and close monitoring, I was able to restore the weight in about two months.

About a month after my surgery, I was cleared to start driving again. I placed a small pillow between my incision and the seat belt. I felt happy to pick the twins up from school and drive them around locally. While I spent most of March resting at home, I enjoyed short outings and time with friends followed by cozy evenings at home with my family. I got out for walks every day that the weather allowed and gradually increased the time walking outside. Though I tired easily, I slowly but surely was able to do more routine activities at home. I was making progress!

Rebecca came home for a March visit over her spring break from graduate school and we all enjoyed attending Matthew's All State Band Concert. At the end of the month, I had my final appointment with Dr. Bandera. She cleared me to slowly resume my activities.

On April 9, a beautiful spring day, Jeff hit some tennis balls with me. I was so happy to be back on the court. Many people had asked me "how will you ever manage not playing tennis for two months?" My response was "I don't have ovarian cancer." I felt tremendous gratitude for my health and for the love and support given to me through two months of rest and healing.

As April went on, I gradually increased my time on the court and by the end of the month, I was able to play a competitive match!

This experience, surviving major surgery, was a powerful reminder that I have only one body, so I need to take care of it. I did everything I needed to do to take care of my body so that I could heal and resume my life. I nurtured my body with rest and nourished my body with food. I returned to my pre-surgery weight by April wanting to feel not only healthy, but strong.

In recovery from my eating disorder, I learned to negate negative body image thoughts by focusing on what my body could do. My appreciation deepened for what my body could do when it was healthy and strong. My ED recovery grew even stronger after my surgery experience. I was fiercely determined to be as strong and as healthy as possible. This experience also strengthened my recovery by reinforcing my commitment to self-care, not only for my body, but also for my mind and spirit. I never again wanted to deprive my body of what it needed on a daily basis. Grace guided me every step of the way, helping me to regain my strength and needed weight. At no time did ED interfere. I needed food for proper nourishment for strength and healing. I listened to my body instead of ED.

Return to good physical health and my ED recovery went hand in hand. I felt immense gratitude after being reminded profoundly that each day of life and health is truly a gift. I had put my faith in God and got through a major life challenge without using ED as a coping tool. When my health returned, I believed that my recovery was stronger than ever.

I can't help but compare this experience with a physical illness to my experience with mental illness. With my surgery and cancer-scare, I received much care, love, and support every step of the way. With my eating disorder, on the other hand, I had felt shame, secrecy, and very little support or understanding.

My surgery experience, one of my most difficult challenges, taught me important lessons. With renewed gratitude and appreciation for a healthy body and my life, my ED recovery would grow stronger with many gifts of recovery just around the bend.

CHAPTER XVII

———

A Time of Transition

The euphoric gratitude that followed the surgery propelled my eating disorder recovery forward. Embracing the lessons from that most challenging experience, I considered myself as recovered from my eating disorder.

This greater appreciation for my health and well-being, strengthened by a commitment to being my healthiest self, helped me to cross the recovery line that Grace always said was within reach. I wanted Grace, and Emily, to see me as recovered.

During this time in mid-2017, I continued to see Emily weekly. I needed that safe space with her to continue to unravel my layers of suppressed emotions. Without an eating disorder to numb the emotions, tears flowed more easily. I was unaware then, but this was part of the hard work of recovery. While the marker of Grace's finish line was, in essence, the restoration of nutrition, the "feeling the feelings" stage in connecting with my healthy self was just beginning. Only after the body is weight-restored and the brain is functioning properly, can this difficult leg of the recovery journey begin to unfold. I had learned how to fuel my body, but now I was learning to cope with the overflowing and at times overwhelming emotions. The proverbial dam had broken and there was no way to hold the water back. This is where my recovery was now, learning to feel and tolerate a range of emotions.

Grace travelled often, but we met when she was in town to ensure that my weight was stable. During the five years when my eating disorder controlled me, I had become dependent on her. She had helped me with much more than nutrition and meal plans. We talked about everything and she was the first person with whom I could be truly vulnerable. I treasured my connection with her and efforts to become less dependent on her care were emotionally challenging.

When I first suggested to Grace that I discontinue the daily emails in early May 2017, she said, "Let's not change what is working." Typically, there is little to no communication between a patient and their professional support from one appointment to the next, but Grace gave me that extra care and support without which I may not have progressed so soon or as far in my recovery. She was always just a quick text or email away. She allowed me to express what I was experiencing or feeling in the moment, rather than waiting until the next appointment. One particular incident comes to mind.

> *I am going out in a little while with tennis friends and when I was getting ready, ED was being very cruel. I tried on many different outfits and each time ED told me I looked too fat.*

Grace was there for me when I needed her.

> *It must be so hard to have ED in the room when you are trying to get dressed. ED needs corrective lens surgery. Feel free to vent any time.*

At that point, Grace was one of the few people with whom I could share details of my struggles with ED.

I felt that I should no longer be so dependent, yet I accepted and appreciated Grace's generous care and support. Emily strongly believed that it was time to "take off the training wheels" and learn to "ride" on my own. I was confident riding with my training wheels and had no idea that when they suddenly came off, I would fall. I didn't have the opportunity to learn how to keep my balance while still having "a guiding hand behind my seat."

Grace soon limited my emails to once a week and this new boundary was harder to accept than I thought it would be. It illustrated how dependent I had become on Grace during the past six years. On many levels her care and support had sustained me. Grace's expertise in nutrition and her inspiring words provided daily motivation in recovery.

I also admired Grace as a person. She and her husband seemed to have a healthy work/life balance and appeared to live life to the fullest while each remained invested in their meaningful careers. I loved our conversations about life, about faith, and about living our best lives. We shared inspiring quotes and both loved the beach. Grace would email sunrise pictures from the balcony of her Florida condo which directly overlooked the ocean. The sunrises brought feelings of peace no matter what else was happening. I made sure to get up early to experience the majestic sunrise on our family beach vacations. I learned from Grace that feeling at peace is not black or white. Rather, life is messy and complicated, yet I could still experience peace amidst the chaos. Until then, my anxiety had kept me from feeling at peace, but Grace connected me to the concept of calmness and reassured me that I deserved to experience it. This was one of the many gifts I received from Grace during our time together.

The year 2017 continued to be a time of transition. The once a week emails transitioned to emails whenever I had something important that I wanted to share. Since our conversations went far beyond food and nutrition and since ED's voice had become much quieter, I didn't always know what was okay to share with Grace. She assured me that I could share anything I wanted. I did not want to lose our connection, but tried to keep the emails to a minimum.

During in-person meetings with Grace in 2017, I became extremely emotional at times. The tears were flowing freely. Looking back, I believe I became too much for Grace. She was a dietitian, not a therapist, although she had originally encouraged me to be open, authentic and vulnerable. She said I needed to "feel the feelings and be free." I now think she would have preferred that my overwhelming emotions flowed elsewhere.

The training wheels connecting me to Grace definitely needed to come off. Without completely understanding why at the time, contributing to the tears was my fear of losing Grace and not having the care and support on which I had grown dependent. As a result of my upbringing, I equated vulnerability and dependency with weakness. But Grace had taught me that these human qualities were essential for recovery. I had let Grace in and she connected with a side of me that few people had seen. Throughout the process of letting my guard down and sharing more, I never thought about ever having to say goodbye. Grace reassured me many times that I would not have to say goodbye.

In hindsight, the training wheels, or easing of my reliance on Grace, should have been raised earlier, and gradually, to encourage independence and maintenance of my self-balance. The reality was that my dependency on Grace went way beyond the email support and I became terrified of losing her care and understanding. I did not yet have the confidence needed to "ride" on my own.

In the fall of 2017, I expressed to Grace in an email what she meant to me.

> *I had no idea when I first came to you that you would become one of the biggest and most important and positive influences in my life. You have literally been with me every step of the way, through all the steps forward and steps backward. You have helped me through illness, injury, and surgery and the extra challenges for my recovery which they presented. You have listened and listened and have given me a level of care and support that I have never had before. I have also never before let anyone in like I let you in. Knowing you will always think of me as a friend means so much. I am relieved I never have to say goodbye forever. There are no words to adequately express my gratitude. You have endured so many of my complicated and difficult emotions and responded to well over a thousand emails. The journey continues and I look forward to finding out where it will take me.*

The challenge would be to find the right balance between sharing openly and honestly, without being too dependent. Grace encouraged me to express my feelings but I was unable to do so without tears. We had spent time as friends outside the office and had managed to keep our professional relationship separate. I had even spent a long weekend with Grace at her Florida condo. It was truly wonderful having that time with her, but looking back, I must have feared professional scrutiny of this invitation because I intentionally withheld the details of my trip from Emily. Nonetheless, I enjoyed the weekend and in my mind it confirmed that Grace thought of me as a friend. Now, as there was a decreasing need for our professional relationship, where did that leave us? Grace often reassured me that she would always think of me as a friend. In my vulnerability, I believed her. The more tears I shed, however, the more I felt insecure about our friendship. Any discussion about our relationship revolved around my tears and my words. Right then, it would have been helpful to know more about what Grace was thinking.

Emily thought that my ED was clinging by a thread to justify continued dependency on Grace's care and support. My healthy-self wanted ED to be gone completely, so that the professional relationship would end and our friendship could remain. Grace had said she looked forward to the day when we could meet for lunch and talk as friends. Yet, my over-dependency on her care and support made the transition to friends more difficult. I could not have understood or appreciated the complexities at the time.

In hindsight, the professional relationship ought to have concluded as soon as I no longer needed nutrition support. However, the food was only one facet of my recovery work with Grace. As we approached the end of our work together, I was unable to hold back the tears in our meetings, and Grace sensed the need for Emily's intervention.

> *I believe there is one more area we need to explore and unravel. I am at a loss over how to help but I think Emily can help us figure it out.*

Grace compared our situation to that of a child leaving home for college.

> *It's growth and separation and it can be scary and uncomfortable for everyone. But the child will grow and mature and become independent. We will figure this out with help and support. You are not alone.*

Emily never was given the opportunity to help us to figure this out. In early 2018, Grace went away for a month. She said there would be no communication between us during this time away. While I missed the connection, it was necessary. When Grace returned, our "discharge plan" was in place. We met outside her office setting and still talked about whatever I needed to express. I appreciated meeting in this way but had to be mindful of not becoming tearful in the public coffee shop setting. Our professional relationship officially ended with a meeting at Grace's office in June 2018. Though we may have skipped important steps that could have eased the transition, Grace nonetheless played a significant role in my recovery and was present for one of the best days in my life. The details of this empowering experience in May 2018, and other gifts of recovery, are explored in the next chapter.

CHAPTER XVIII

Gifts of Recovery

After recovering from surgery and returning to tennis and my normal routine, I had a deeper appreciation for the gift of an ordinary day. I had restored the weight I lost post-surgery and was maintaining a relatively healthy body size. Recovery from my eating disorder grew stronger daily by nourishing my body, mind, and spirit, fueling my exercise sufficiently, and taking care of my own needs.

As my healthy voice strengthened, ED's voice grew quieter. I treasured connection with people with whom I could be my authentic self. I was able to be fully present in my life. With my brain not consumed by thoughts about food and exercise all day and every day, I could appreciate the beauty of the world around me such as noticing the way the sun sparkled on the water on my frequent beach walks. I could enjoy simple pleasures and time with my family and close friends. I no longer felt guilty about time devoted to self-care. Recognizing and meeting my own needs was not selfish. I was learning to listen to my body, enjoying food, and eating in restaurants.

Occasionally I would hear from ED, but now I was better equipped to respond in a way that prioritized my health, with kindness and compassion.

A big challenge during this time was maintaining strong recovery against a backdrop of attitudes in my household which prioritized perfectionism and productivity. I was learning to relax more and feel more at peace but this was hard at times when surrounded by type-A personalities. I am still learning how my recovered self fits in.

Recovery is never perfect and I continued to feel a connection between exercise and food intake. As always, playing tennis made me feel good about myself and reduced anxiety. The exercise also increased my appetite which made eating easier. The biggest revelation in recovery was that I could take days off from exercise without restriction and still enjoy meals out or treats like ice cream.

While in the depths of my eating disorder, my treatment team encouraged me to look for a support group that could be another resource in my recovery journey. Ironically, though I felt comfortable facilitating a long-standing Bereavement Group in my community, the thought of being a group participant made me feel uncomfortable. From January through March of 2015, I attended an eight-week support group for women over 35. There was nothing like this in Rhode Island so I travelled for over an hour, often contending with traffic and snow, to attend this group offered by the Multi-Service Eating Disorder Association (MEDA), just outside Boston. MEDA provides valuable education, resources, and support for people suffering from eating disorders and their loved ones.

I loved the inspirational quotes they posted on the wall in MEDA's warm and welcoming environment. As a result, I started my own book of quotes. This sounds like a simple self-help strategy, but these quotes were very helpful on difficult days. My book included inspiring quotes from MEDA, Grace, and from social media. I continue to collect and add to my book any meaningful quote I see from a variety of sources.

While at one of the group's weekly meetings, I saw a flyer on the wall for "Hope and Inspiration." This was a free monthly event where someone who had recovered from an eating disorder could share their story and answer questions. Held in a room at MEDA on the first Saturday of every month, the event was open to the community. I decided to attend one Saturday and thought, *"Won't it be amazing if one day I can be the recovery speaker at MEDA's 'Hope and Inspiration.'"*

During the summer of 2017, when feeling good about my recovery, I met with a clinician at MEDA to discuss the possibility of speaking at "Hope and

Inspiration." She knew me from my attendance at the eight-week support group and had noticed the glow on my face when describing the progress I had made since my group attendance, and how my recent surgery experience had propelled my recovery forward. We set a date for the following year, May 5, 2018, for me to be the "Hope and Inspiration" speaker.

During the fall of 2017, though busy coaching my high school tennis team to the State Championship Finals, I used any free time to start preparing my recovery story.

I was in my early 50s at this point with many chapters of life behind me. I needed to get in touch with, feel, and write about the difficult experiences and challenges over that time. I wrote for the first time about my parents' divorce, their cancer battles and deaths, the development of my eating disorder, and my recovery. I wanted to heal on a deep level and give hope and inspiration to others. I wrote my story over the course of three months, writing for a few hours at a time. There were many tears and my blocks of writing were often determined by how much I could tolerate emotionally.

May 5, 2018 was one of the most impactful days of my life. I was MEDA's "Hope and Inspiration" speaker on a beautiful spring Saturday. Four very special people in the audience were supporting me: Jeff, Grace, and two close friends. One of the four said later that I spoke as if giving the Valedictorian's speech at a graduation. I felt on top of the world. There was barely a dry eye in the room when I finished. I will always be grateful for this powerful experience, one which I could only wish for in the winter of 2015 when I first attended the support group at MEDA.

In 2018, this was my new reality. I was fortunate to share my story at many treatment centers in and around Boston. At all levels of care, I loved answering questions about my journey as well as meeting and connecting with many caring clinicians. Each time I shared my story, I felt empowered, authentic, happy, and strong. I felt like I was truly making a difference in people's lives. As a result, my speaking experiences were definitely one of the greatest gifts of recovery.

In addition to speaking at eating disorder treatment centers, I was honored to be one of two featured speakers at MEDA's Breakfast in the Fall of 2018. At the Breakfast, I shared a short version of my story in front of 200 people at MEDA's biggest annual fundraiser. Six months later, in April 2019,

I shared the short version of my story at the Rhode Island National Eating Disorders Association Walk. The Walk raises money for and awareness about eating disorders.

My story, emphasizing that recovery from an eating disorder is possible, even in mid-life, was also shared on several well-known blogs and websites in the eating disorder world. All of these speaking opportunities and seeing my story in print continue to empower my self-belief and strengthen my recovery.

Most recently, I have been providing peer support, mentoring, and co-leading support groups for people who are struggling with eating disorders. There is now a place in Providence, Rhode Island, "be Collaborative Care," which offers excellent clinicians and an intensive out-patient program (IOP) for eating disorders. I am thrilled that Rhode Island has such a facility, and I look forward to doing more of this important work in the future.

The gifts of my recovery have been more than I could have envisioned when I could not see a way out of my illness. In recovery, I have learned to use healthier coping skills to deal with life's stresses to avoid regressing to eating disorder behaviors. Life will always present challenges and being mindful of reaching into that proverbial toolbox and digging deep is vital to resist reverting to the eating disorder. Inner strength in difficult situations means reaching out for support, making connections, acknowledging vulnerability, and being extra kind and loving to myself.

Recovery is rarely linear and relapse is common no matter how strong recovery has been. I am no exception. My experience illustrates the importance of admitting to a struggle and seeking the appropriate professional help. Relapse is a normal part of recovery, not something to be ashamed of or embarrassed about experiencing. Unfortunately, I experienced a setback in late 2018 despite years of hard work in recovery.

In September 2018, three months after my last professional appointment with Grace, her husband died suddenly and unexpectedly. He was a wonderful man whom I had met several times. I felt shattered for Grace and her family, and I attended both the wake and the funeral mass.

As I would have done for anyone I cared about, I reached out with texts, a supportive email, a card, and a special little book about grief. I had years of experience with grief and loss, both personally and quasi-professionally. I had supported many friends and acquaintances in their time of need and many were grateful for my support. I wanted to support Grace in any way that would help. I knew I couldn't take away her pain and heartache, but I wanted her to know how much I cared.

She initially seemed to appreciate my expressions of care and support, but then, two months after her husband's death, I received a text from her asking me to "stop all communication until our paths cross at some future point." I was devastated and immediately looked at myself to blame. Maybe I had reached out too soon or texted her too often. I had sensed during the summer that Grace was not completely comfortable with a friendship, but it had also been a very busy time for her and we hadn't spent any significant time together. Yet, here I was, shattered beyond words by this sudden rejection.

All I wanted was to fit into her life in some casual way and now she was stopping all communication between us with no opportunity to truly understand why. I respected her wishes and did not respond but the pain ran deep. I felt like I needed to hurt myself to gain relief from the pain. Those thoughts scared me, but in no way would I have ever acted upon them. I felt no anger. All I felt was overwhelming sadness.

I did not intentionally go back to my eating disorder though I felt ED was sitting "nearby" offering to help me numb these intensely difficult emotions. I was neither restricting nor over-exercising to cope with the unbearable pain. I needed to connect with understanding friends who could listen and support me as I expressed my feelings. I tried but the reality was that few truly understood the importance of my relationship with Grace, her role in my recovery, and her impact on my life. Subconsciously, I began internalizing the hurt and sadness. Though consumed by the crushing emotional upheaval, I continued my daily living, fully engaged in the roles I cherished.

I thought about Grace often and yearned for answers. I reread her text many times. I wondered if this was the "good-bye forever" I had feared, or whether this was a temporary break while she grieved the devastating loss of her husband. I continued to blame myself, incapable of feeling anger and letting her go. I didn't understand how she could go from being initially receptive to my support and saying that I could come by when her extended family left, to cutting off all communication. I was left with many questions and few answers. I was filled with sadness and self-blame. I cared too much.

Though I had worked hard for many years to eradicate ED from my life, he was lurking just below the surface trying to help me cope on the most subtle level.

I didn't realize it at the time, but this loss triggered the deep wounds my parents had unintentionally inflicted upon me as a result of their own issues. I thought writing my recovery story had helped me to heal those deepest wounds, but this loss touched my core, another knife in my heart. I did not comprehend why or how I had given Grace so much power over me. I now needed to grieve the loss of a relationship that was still not fully understood. It was difficult for Jeff and my closest friends to see me so sad and hurting so deeply. They would have preferred for me to feel angry, as they did, and let her go. I was an expert at internalizing feelings. It was what I knew best.

I regretted letting myself be vulnerable with Grace. I regretted letting myself become deeply dependent on her care and support. I associated many gifts of recovery with Grace and now I was left with unbearable pain and a need to pause my focus on the wonderful places my recovery journey had taken me over the past year.

The reality was I could no longer ignore the weight loss noticed by Emily, Jeff, and my closest friends. Emily wanted me to meet with a new dietitian but this immediately felt like failure to me. Didn't I already know by now how to fuel my body properly? Ultimately, I agreed to see a new dietitian, but I would not let my guard down. My "I'll try to eat more" was clearly not working, but any recommended interventions felt like punishment.

I eventually figured out two other factors that significantly contributed to my weight loss. They may seem less important than the emotional upheaval following Grace's text, but actually these factors were more directly connected to the weight loss.

With recovery came the freedom to eat what I wanted, when I wanted, and without accountability. This freedom felt great! But Grace had always warned me that if I ate only to my appetite, I would lose weight. I had always had a hard time eating when not hungry. Well, clearly what I thought was freedom was not enough to fuel my body sufficiently. As an athlete, I needed even more fuel to support my competitive tennis. Here I was not depriving myself or ignoring hunger. I was eating meals and snacks, and taking more days off from exercise, but I was not eating unless feeling hungry. Grace was absolutely correct and I had not heeded her warning. The result was weight loss I could not afford.

Another contributing factor to my weight loss was indirectly connected to my surgically induced menopause following my hysterectomy in 2017. I had read that menopause could increase cholesterol levels. When my blood work revealed the highest number I had seen shortly after Grace's fit husband died suddenly of a heart attack, I was shocked and upset. Even though my doctor reassured me that my overall numbers put me at extremely low cardiac risk, the number became lodged in my brain as something to be concerned about. This worry created heightened anxiety rather than a return to ED, yet the cheese and eggs I had eaten freely now became food items of concern. Unfortunately, this led to an exaggerated focus on "clean" eating. I thought I was being my healthiest self, but my reluctance to eat certain foods because of cholesterol fears was contributing to my weight loss.

I respected the recommendations of Emily and my new dietitian which came from a place of professional knowledge and care. The self-awareness gained in recovery helped me identify the contributing factors to the unintended weight loss. Decisions made going forward regarding food choices would need to be based on my body's needs. Food was and always will be my medicine.

The setback with my weight loss was upsetting and challenging, yet it helped me refocus my efforts on physical and emotional health.

The impact, however, of Grace's text on my emotional health could not be minimized. Healing required delving deeper to understand my reaction to her words and to learn how to move forward despite the crushing sadness. *A setback, whether physical or emotional, can be a gift of recovery in disguise. As long as lessons are learned with each twist and turn, recovery continues to get stronger.*

So here I was with my weight at its lowest point in years and my emotional well-being shattered by the power over me of a simple text. I will always be grateful to Emily for helping me "unpack" this complicated and completely disguised "gift" of recovery. In my mind, using the word "gift" could only be an extreme misnomer. In my mind, Grace's request to stop all communication could in no way be construed as a gift. My biggest fear was coming true. I had to say "goodbye" to Grace, but the reality was made worse by not actually getting to say "goodbye." This lack of closure made the situation more heart-wrenching.

As always, there was never enough time with Emily. Many sessions were spent talking about my relationship with Grace, what mistakes she made, and the impact on me. Emily would never have let me ride with the training wheels on for so long. Yes, dependency and vulnerability were necessary for my recovery, but Grace had provided a level of care and support far beyond the standards her professional role dictated.

Grace had only good intentions and I will always be grateful for her important role in my recovery. However, as an experienced professional, she went beyond the boundaries that typically characterize the professional relationship between a dietitian and client. Grace never would have intentionally inflicted pain upon me.

Emily helped me to understand that though Grace should have known, she did not understand the impact of her ways. I had interpreted and internalized Grace's care, support and friendship as real and enduring. I had taken her words to heart. Her words had motivated me through recovery and helped me immensely. However, she had left me in a precarious state. I wanted to hold on to her care and support, the depth of which I had never experienced before, yet I also wanted to embrace a friendship that I believed would survive and thrive with the end of our professional relationship.

I have learned the hard way that this was not possible. Jeff and my closest friends wanted me to emotionally disconnect from Grace completely. For this reason, I felt I could no longer talk about what had happened with them, because I didn't agree with what they said. Emily patiently listened and listened as I talked about Grace, overanalyzed her text, and shed tears over this loss. Her tremendous skills as a therapist and her understanding of all aspects of my journey with Grace helped me immeasurably along this difficult path to healing and understanding. This process continues and I am deeply grateful for Emily's insight and professional compassion.

2019 brought a state high school tennis championship in May and Rebecca and Brandon's beautiful wedding in June, yet sadness followed me through most of the year as a result of Grace's conscious rejection. This painful event, however, became an important and necessary piece of my recovery. To continue the bike metaphor, the training wheels eventually came off completely. I fell and sustained serious injury. But the healing process has brought new skills and a deeper level of understanding. The scars from my injury remain, but I am riding on my own and balancing just fine. When I start to veer one way or the other, I use the skills I have learned. I reach out for support, I feel the feelings, I learn important lessons, and I keep riding forward. There may be more bumps on my path, and likely I will fall again, but with each "fall," the self-awareness, determination, and perseverance will enable me to keep riding.

Do I still hold onto a glimmer of hope that our paths will indeed cross at some future point? I definitely do, because that is who I am. I will never stop caring about Grace, but I will no longer give her the power she once had over me. She, like me, is human and imperfect.

I am emerging from this recovery detour stronger than before. I am determined to live my best life and use healthy coping skills for handling anxiety, challenges, and any "cuts or bruises," big and small.

Recovery brings the opportunity to experience life in new ways and to appreciate the gifts. Relationships replace eating disorders, and I am truly grateful for the people in my life who understand me, support me, and appreciate me for who I am.

Recovery, like life, doesn't have to be perfect to be wonderful. I savor the gifts of recovery as I continue my life. One of the exciting tasks going forward is figuring out in my 50s who I am without my eating disorder.

I remain a work in progress and food remains my medicine. Emily will continue to help me to fine tune my skills and listen to me without judgment. With her, I have the professional care and consistency I can depend on as I continually strive to be my healthiest self in mind, body, and spirit. Life will always be messy and complicated, but the ride goes on.

CHAPTER XIX

———

Inner Peace

A silver lining of the COVID-19 pandemic in 2020 was the gift of time to write my memoir. I looked inward to examine my life and put it into words. My purpose was to heal on the deepest level possible and, through sharing my story, to help and inspire others who are struggling with similar challenges.

Jeff often told me that my life story had the makings of a book. I never thought seriously about taking on a project of this magnitude until best-selling author and eating disorder recovery advocate, Jenni Schaefer, told me that my recovery story could become a book if I were willing to invest the time and effort to expand my story. With Jeff's encouragement and the professional guidance and support of Dr. June Alexander, my memoir has become a reality.

Every day I feel tremendous gratitude for the abundance of blessings in my life and the happiness and joy they bring. Through the process of writing my memoir, I have a deeper understanding of how my many challenges have shaped me. I am also grateful for the important lessons these challenges have taught me.

Reading through old diaries, from my childhood and into adulthood, in preparation for writing my memoir gave me a lens through which I could see myself at different life stages. These diaries provide unequivocal evidence that the threads of my anxiety, depression, and eating disorder were woven throughout the tapestry of my life stemming from my parents' acrimonious divorce in 1970.

My sad inner child craved the unconditional love that my parents were not always able to give in the way that I needed due to their own issues. I believe they did the best they could, but their behavior profoundly affected my emotional development. My parents took their animosity toward each other out on me. Slowly but surely, I developed anxiety, fears, and was unable to express outwardly how each parent made me feel.

Mom modeled for me after her divorce that, despite this difficult life-changing event, we were expected to go on with our lives as if nothing had happened. I was neither able to express sadness, nor nurture the sad inner child. Without permission or encouragement to feel, I began to internalize all negative feelings and emotions.

Mom raised my sister and me to focus on our blessings. Appreciation and gratitude are certainly important, but I did not learn how to cope with challenges in a healthy way. My false sense of "inner strength" developed, regrettably, at the expense of my mental health. I perceived myself as being strong which I equated to being positive and unemotional. Mom's rigid and controlling nature made it difficult for me to be fully human—that is, to be imperfect, vulnerable, and emotional. My inner strength was not based on resiliency, but rather was focused on persevering and internalizing any difficult emotions along the way.

My battle with myself has permeated my life. Unable to tolerate risk, failure, negative affect, vulnerability, or weakness of any kind, I would be wracked with guilt for even thinking anything negative. When each of my parents died, I thought I was supposed to focus on being grateful for the two special years I had with each of them prior to their deaths, rather than allow myself to grieve and feel the immense sadness. The two good years that I had with each of them were indeed gifts. However, failing to acknowledge my grief and internalizing the pain affected my emotional health. I learned the hard way that I couldn't suppress all the pain. The effort to do so led to feelings of rage, anxiety, and depression. I battled myself and experienced tremendous feelings of guilt whenever the negative feelings and emotions tried to escape.

The development of an eating disorder in mid-life became my catalyst for healing. I embarked on an exploration of self along a difficult path which required getting in touch with layers of suppressed emotions.

Besides identifying the emotions, I needed to develop new, healthier ways of thinking. Traits I had equated with weakness were actually necessary for resiliency and strength. The sad inner child who craved unconditional love needed to be cared for and have her needs met. The self-awareness that emerged during my recovery allowed me to recognize and understand that I have needs and it's okay to meet them. The eating disorder was the culmination of my challenges. Recovery and the examination of my life through old diaries confirmed the neglected and sad inner child. Through ongoing nurturing of my mind, body, and spirit, I am healing that sad inner child by meeting her need for unconditional love.

My childhood experiences turned me into a shy, sensitive, and caring woman. I knew how to care for others' needs, but not my own. I originally wanted to be a child psychologist to help children whose parents were divorced. I did not follow that path, but I did take the chaplain's advice about helping others with their grief and became a hospice volunteer. I am proud of the Bereavement Group that I started in my community in 2012. This was intended to be a six-week group focused on coping with grief and the holidays. It has developed into an ongoing group with many people attending for varying periods—weeks, months, or even years. Men and women of all ages, and with different losses, come together to support one another in a welcoming, and non-judgmental way. Channeling my own grief into this meaningful work has further assisted my ongoing healing.

Similarly, I have taken the experience of my eating disorder and made it count in a positive way by helping others. I mentor women in mid-life through texts, emails, and phone calls. I also lead peer support groups where people struggling with an eating disorder can talk to someone who "gets it." By helping others, my own recovery gets stronger. Similarly, every time I share my recovery story, I am helping others in an empowering way.

I am grateful for both my childhood tennis career and my return to tennis in adulthood which led to my coaching career. As a child, tennis provided a healthy outlet for emotions I was unable to express. Tennis provided a sense of purpose and I worked hard to achieve goals. I gained self-confidence along the way. Tennis created the opportunity to travel and to make lifelong friendships. Tennis made me feel special and fueled my self-esteem. When I returned to competitive tennis in my 40s, tennis provided wonderful friendships and added to my self-esteem. Unfortunately, tennis also became entwined in my eating disorder.

Putting the eating disorder challenge aside, since 2008, my coaching career has provided opportunity to be a positive role model. I ensure the athletes who I coach know I am another adult in their lives who cares about them not only as tennis players, but as people. I care about my players on and off the court and try to teach them life lessons such as self-belief, working hard to achieve goals, and never giving up. I have celebrated big wins, helped my athletes to learn from losses, hosted ice cream parties, shared inspirational quotes, and met wonderful coaching colleagues, many of whom have become friends. I have helped players through challenges in their own lives such as mental health issues, physical injuries, parents' divorce, and break-ups with boyfriends. I have also had the pleasure of coaching all three of my children. My second career as a high school tennis coach did not require my law degree, but it has been an extremely fulfilling endeavor, one that I continue to enjoy. Making a difference in the lives of others adds meaning to my own. I am proud of my coaching career on and off the court.

Going forward, I will continue to appreciate the blessings and savor each day free from ED's control. I am at peace with my past, and excited for the continued discovery of who I am without my eating disorder. I will continue to practice being loving and kind to myself, providing compassion to that sad inner child. I no longer seek approval from anyone but myself. My parents did the best they could and I appreciate the good times and the opportunities they provided. I am grateful for my comfortable childhood home, a privileged education, my tennis career, and many treasured memories.

Jeff came into my life in law school in 1987, and he has made my dreams come true—a happy marriage, a home in the suburbs, and three precious children. Rebecca is happily married to Brandon, living and teaching history in Virginia, and will soon complete her Doctorate in American History. Alexis and Matthew are happy college students, on the bridge from childhood to adulthood. Jeff and I are enjoying more time together and post-pandemic we look forward to traveling and visiting more with friends and family near and far. Eventually, we hope to become grandparents.

I have done my best raising our children and giving them the unconditional love and support I wish that I had while growing up. I have encouraged them to share their feelings and express their emotions. I made parenting mistakes along the way and I know there were things I could have done better, but my children know they are loved and hopefully they know I am human and have tried my best.

A book resonated with me when emerging from the depths of my grief following Mom's death. Carol Hamblet Adams, *My Beautiful Broken Shell*, published by Harvest House Publishers in 2002, uses beach imagery to beautifully depict strength and healing. The author likens herself with her broken heart to the broken scallop shell she discovers on the beach. This broken shell represents strength and survival. The shell had *"fought hard to keep from being totally crushed by the pounding surf."*

Hamblet Adams explains that we can learn from the symbolism of this imperfect shell.

> *Broken shells mean lots of tears . . . lots of pain . . . lots of struggle . . .*
> *but they are also valuable for teaching faith, courage, and strength.*

I have read this book aloud to my bereavement group through the years and it always elicits comfort and strength in the midst of their grief.

My Beautiful Broken Shell now speaks to me in a new way. I perceive that shell as me on my recovery journey from my eating disorder. Hamblet Adams' words, through beach imagery, illustrate the key components to my healing. The broken shell represents authenticity.

> *As I look at my beautiful broken shell, I see that it has nothing to hide.*
> *It doesn't pretend to be perfect or whole. . . . Its brokenness is clear for*
> *everyone to see.*

In addition to authenticity, vulnerability and connection have been essential to my recovery. Once again, this is splendidly illustrated by Hamblet Adams in one of the short prayers in her book.

May I give myself permission to hurt . . . to cry . . . to be human. May I have the courage to risk sharing my feelings with others so that I may receive support and encouragement along the way.

Recovery required that I give myself permission to feel all feelings and emotions, both positive and negative, without guilt. I am no longer at war with myself and have learned to embrace authenticity, vulnerability, and connection with those who understand me and accept me for who I am. I will continue to be a work in progress while engaging in more self-compassion and self-care. In the late 1990s, when I began attending Church and going on long solo bike rides, self-care was not in my vocabulary. I felt guilty taking time for myself away from my responsibilities. Now 20 years later, self-care comes with no guilt attached and is accepted as necessary for my health and well-being. I sincerely hope that the future threads in my life's tapestry will be woven from a place of health, happiness, and inner peace.

Like a piece of sea glass on the sand, I too have been transformed by the turbulent seas. My past will remain an important part of who I am, but difficult experiences no longer cast a dark shadow on my ability to manage life's stressors. Self-awareness is now the root of my resiliency. Accordingly, with self-care, love and compassion, I am living a healthier life in mind, body, and spirit.

With resilience comes a new level of self-awareness and freedom. I am no longer constrained by ED. I am free, free to be me, free to use my voice, free to connect with others authentically, and free to be fully present in life. Walking along the beach looking for sea glass embodies the joy of discovery. I continue to discover who I am without my eating disorder and savor every moment of this journey toward healing and lasting inner peace. There will always be storms, but I am now a skilled sailor and am better equipped to adjust the sails. And, I am strong and resilient, like the sea glass on the sand.

I feel most at peace by the ocean, whether watching the sunrise, beachcombing, or enjoying the sunset. It is often when I am feeling most at peace that my emotions rise to the surface. I do my best thinking and feeling at the beach and sometimes the tears stream down my face. I am free to feel my feelings with no shame or guilt.

When watching the sunrise from the beach, there is a moment when "the orange ball" begins to emerge from where the sky meets the ocean. This moment marks the dawning of a new day, bringing daylight to the darkness of the previous night. For me, the orange ball also symbolizes hope—hope, for widespread vaccination against COVID-19—and the light we need to emerge from the 2020 pandemic.

There is nothing more authentic than writing and sharing a memoir. I am literally now an open book. I hope that readers will relate in some way and be inspired along their own journey. It's never too late to be a work in progress.

REFERENCE:

Hamblet Adams, C (2002) My Beautiful Broken Shell Eugene, Oregon: Harvest House Publishers.

ABOUT THE AUTHOR

First time author, Betsy Brenner has been coaching high school tennis since 2008 in Barrington, Rhode Island. She was a nationally ranked junior player, played division one college tennis, and still plays competitively.

Betsy facilitates a longstanding bereavement group in her local community, and for many years worked as a hospice volunteer and speaker on grief and loss. More recently, Betsy has been an eating disorder recovery speaker, peer support mentor, and support group co-leader. Her recovery story has been shared widely on many eating disorder blogs and websites.

Betsy received her Bachelor's Degree in Psychology from Brown University in 1985 and her Juris Doctorate from American University Law School in 1990. She was a hospital attorney for over a decade before leaving the practice of law to focus on raising her children and meaningful volunteer activities. Originally from Rochester, New York, she and her husband Jeff have resided in Barrington, Rhode Island for 30 years and are the proud parents of three grown children.

WEBSITE: www.betsybrenner.com
EMAIL: betsybrenner3@gmail.com
FACEBOOK: The Longest Match
INSTAGRAM: @betsybrennerauthor

- think
- slow
- think

42789443R00139